ART AND RELIGION

IN THERA

Reconstructing a Bronze Age

Society

by

Nannó Marinatos

*To the memory of my father
who died as a result of a fatal
accident while excavating Akrotiri*

NANNO MARINATOS

ART AND RELIGION

IN THERA

RECONSTRUCTING A BRONZE AGE SOCIETY

ATHENS

ISBN 960-7310-27-6

Table of Contents

PREFACE

Since their discovery the Theran frescoes have been the subject of much study. Usually, however, they are discussed as works of art detached from their pictorial and spatial context. This approach is fruitful as far as art history is concerned but it is inadequate once the question of meaning enters the picture. The significance and purpose of wall paintings can only be perceived if one looks at them in their spatial setting and takes into consideration the finds and architectural features of the rooms in which they were found. In addition, the direction of movement of a figure and its relation to other paintings or architectural features of the room may give us significant clues concerning function.

The purpose of this book is to make a synthesis of the published evidence and to attempt an interpretation of the Theran wall paintings. Although the emphasis is on the art and religion of Akrotiri some observations about its social structure had to be made as they bear directly on the art.

It must be stressed that the present work is not a publication of the material which is a task undertaken by Ch. Doumas and a team of experts. The publication is under way and when the various volumes appear, more light will be thrown on difficult questions. My own conclusions are based on the preliminary reports by Sp. Marinatos (1967-73) and Ch. Doumas (1975-82) and must remain tentative until the final publication of the material. Yet, it seemed worth while to attempt a synthesis even at this stage, if for no other reason than to raise some questions. Since I believe that a visual impression of the entire decorative scheme of a room is necessary for interpretation, I have attempted reconstructions of most painted rooms. Although I think that these restorations are basically correct, they should be considered tentative and we must wait for the exact architectural reconstructions of the publication.

I wish to thank collaborators and colleagues for their valuable comments and discussions; especially Prof. Ch. Doumas for making material and information available to me and for his comments and ideas; Mrs. C. Palyvou for elucidating architectural matters; Prof. E. Davis for discussions on the frescoes; Profs. W. Burkert, E. Harrison and Dr. Ch. Sourvinou-Inwood for comments on the subject of religion. Miss L. Papageorgiou made the reconstructions and Mrs. Brenda Conrad carefully edited the manuscript. Last but not least, I want to thank my husband, Robin Hägg, for his encouragement and help. All the errors remain mine.

Athens, February 1984

CHAPTER I

Introduction: Aims and Methodology

The excavations at Akrotiri have yielded evidence which can potentially revolution-ize our knowledge of the Late Bronze Age. It is not merely because unique frescoes and objects of every day use have been found, but mainly because these objects can be combined together to produce a picture of Theran society. The study of Akrotiri should not involve a mere study of artifacts but of complexes of artifacts and architecture seen together as a unit. The present work will make use of this approach as a methodological tool for the analysis of cult and culture.

A major aim is to understand how the cult at Akrotiri was practiced and its relation to Crete. For this reason reference to Crete is made often; indeed it is sometimes unavoidable to use the term "Minoan" even when describing Theran art or religion. A study or religion involves by necessity a study of the society and a few points have to be made about this. In addition, it is necessary to see Thera in its wider cultural context in the 16th century B.C. Parallels with Crete are instructive and necessary especially for the study of art and religion. Analogies with the Near East and Egypt are necessary and even indispensable. These cultures are better understood than the Aegean civilization and thus further our understanding of the latter.

When drawing analogies between Thera and the Orient my purpose is not to show direct influence. Indeed, sometimes there is a chronological discrepancy. However, analogy is still instructive if we accept that the Aegean and the Orient are closer to each other than they are to our contemporary world. It is my belief that familiarization with the Orient can help us shake off some of our 20th century attitudes which we subconsciously and involuntarily project into the past.

There will be three main methodological principles which will be applied throughout this work. The first is to look for context, the second is to apply analogy; the third is to regard the cultural elements as meaningful signs.

Let us start with the first. Objects and frescoes acquire their meaning in relation to their immediate context, not in isolation. A fresco panel cannot be fully understood if its relation to other frescoes in the room is not explored, nor can its meaning be appreciated if its position in the architectural setting of the room is ignored. The same is true for objects and pottery. Using this method I have identified several shrines at Akrotiri, being careful always to apply the principle of contextual significance. It is perfectly true, for example, that one rhyton or one offering table does not make the room in which it was found a shrine. On the other hand, it is possible to have a shrine without any of the obvious cult equipment which we associate with religion. What we have to look for is **a set of objects** which make sense together as a unit and the function of which can be deduced. For example, if we find several ewers and cups which are imported and of a high quality in a room, we can conclude that drinking was an activity associated with that area. If, in addition, there are tables of offering, small askoi (flasks) which are unguent containers, if there is a stone blossom bowl, etc., then there is a good chance that the drinking was of a ritual nature. This is indicated by the presence of cult implements which have an *a priori* religious character. Now, if there are also frescoes with a religious content in this same room we can be fairly sure that we are dealing with a shrine. It is the combination of the above elements which defines the shrine, not the presence of one or two cult vessels. More specific criteria will be discussed in the next chapter.

The second methodological principle which will be applied is analogy. As mentioned above, this is necessary in order for us to visualize the elusive Minoan and Theran culture and religion. When I use examples from later periods, especially from the Greek Classical period, this is not because I want to prove continuity but to show an analogy. However, I do not wish to deny the possibility of continuity from the Minoan to the Greek period. On the contrary, I am convinced that individual cases of Bronze Age cult survivals can be found. But since the historical and social setting changed, so did the cult patterns. Thus, the very fact of continuity reveals nothing about the nature of the Bronze Age cult. On the other hand, the basic mentality concerning certain phenomena of nature remained the same throughout antiquity and in this case parallels are useful.

Thus, it is better to try and throw light on a case through analogy than to base an argument on continuity. For example, it is not as important to prove that Demeter is a survival of a Minoan mistress of nature as to show that they are both fertility goddesses. Since they share the same capacities as mistresses of nature it is likely that they may have similar cults.

Analogy is useful also in another respect. When dealing with religion we must be aware that it is a discipline in its own right and that knowledge of religious phenomenology is not only helpful but necessary. An archaeologist might not see a connection between a shrine and cooking pots. He will find the presence of the latter puzzling and will be tempted to dismiss the possibility that the room is a shrine. The historian of religion will be aware that cultic meals are present in almost every religion and, thus, he will have no trouble realizing the significance of cooking utensils in a sacral context. Further more, the historian of religion can understand the significance of certain events such as athletic contests. He will know that games and contests are features of religious celebrations, initiation rites and funerary rites.

Use of analogy should be limited, however, since it does not furnish proof but only a possible model. The final proof, if such exists, must come from the contextual analysis.

The third methodological principle is borrowed from semiotics. It involves specifying the place and function of the phenomena and using them to understand the system. For example architectural entities such as houses, squares, building complexes can be analyzed as meaningful signs of a social setting. The plans and

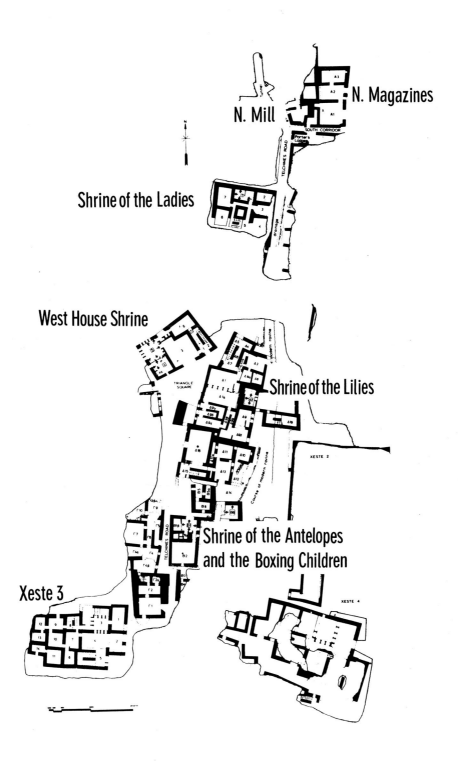

N. Mill

N. Magazines

Shrine of the Ladies

West House Shrine

Shrine of the Lilies

XESTE 2

Shrine of the Antelopes
and the Boxing Children

Xeste 3

XESTE 4

1. Plan of Akrotiri with the location of the shrines.

type of construction give indications of their status and function in the settlement and help us decode the system. This method can also be applied in art. Differentiation of figures by hairstyle, costume, gestures, colour and position give us clues about age, status, office, etc. Thus, decoding the signs is a helpful tool, when used appropriately and with restraint.

In the above I have tried to sketch my methods. This is necessary in a study dealing with religion of a period without written sources where much must appear speculative. Indeed, it is impossible to avoid speculation if any interpretation or reconstruction of rituals is to be attempted at all. But, if speculation is based on a well-defined method some progress can perhaps be made towards understanding the elusive Therans.

2. The mill installation facing a square.

CHAPTER II

The Settlement and its Significance

Architectural Arrangements

Akrotiri was a flourishing town when it was destroyed in c.1500 B.C. It was large and must have had its own harbour. An area of 10.000 m^2 has been excavated so far and it is estimated that this represents about half or less of the total.

Judging from what has been discovered so far, there were three types of buildings at Akrotiri: a) mansions such as Xeste 2,3,4 (fig. 1); b) large independent buildings such as the West House and the House of the Ladies; c) building blocks such as sector A,B,Γ, and Δ. These different types of habitation have their social significance as we shall see.

A street, named by Sp. Marinatos "Telchines' Road", runs in a N-S direction through the settlement (fig. 1). There were probably additional streets E. of it. Three squares are distinguishable on fig. 1. They were important as meeting places for the community and it is noteworthy that adjacent to them there are buildings with an obviously public function. The southernmost square had a mill room (fig. 1,Δ15) on its N. border (fig. 2). The latter had a door opening on to the square through which distribution of flour could take place to the people gathered there. On the S. side of the same square there was a building with a shrine on the upper storey (fig. 1,B1). The latter had a large window through which the public could participate in the ceremonies, especially when the priest or priestess appeared at the window. We can therefore deduce a double function for the square, one economic and one religious.

Towards the N. lies the Triangular Square which had a large building on its N. side, the West House (fig. 3). This building also had a shrine on the upper storey as well as a large window.

It is reasonable to assume that gatherings in front of the West House had a religious character.

Finally, there was apparently a square between the E Façade of sector Δ and the N. façade of Xeste 2 (fig. 1). Although this area is not yet excavated, it is certain that the area was open and devoid of buildings.

The division of the buildings into different categories is proof of social hierarchy. The mansions are the most impressive. They have parallels in Crete and are distinguished by some definite palatial architectural features. One is multiple doors on the crosswalls which result in the creation of large consecutive rooms. The technical term for this arrangement is pier-and-door partition or *polythyron*. Other features are ashlar block façades and "Lustral Basins". The mansions of Akrotiri seem to be clustered in the S. section of the town. There are three of them so far: Xeste 2, 3 and 4.

3. The West House. Note the large window of appearances and the large square.

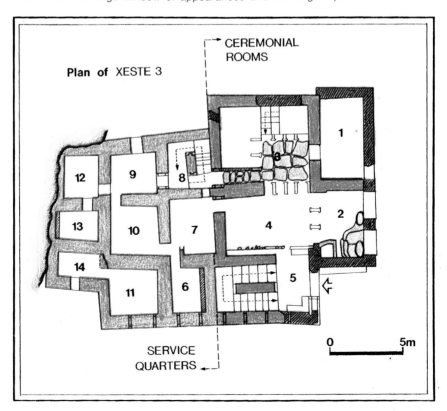

CEREMONIAL ROOMS

Plan of XESTE 3

12 11 10 9 8 7 6 5 4 3 2 1 13 14

SERVICE QUARTERS

0   5m

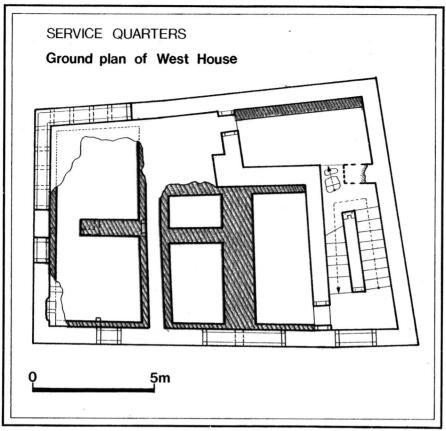

SERVICE QUARTERS

Ground plan of West House

0   5m

4 a-b. *Comparative plans of Xeste 3 and the West House with functional zoning. The service and ceremonial quarters are spread on two storeys in the West House but on one in Xeste 3.*

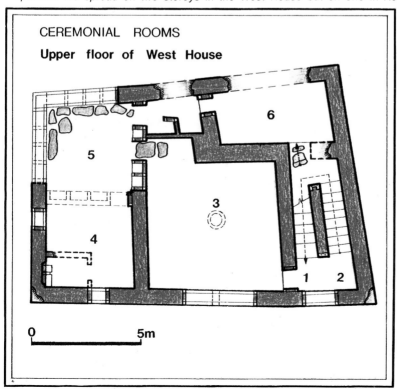

CEREMONIAL ROOMS

Upper floor of West House

6

5

3

4

1   2

0   5m

Xeste 3 (fig. 4a) which is now fully excavated can serve as an example of this type of building. It can be divided into two sections, an eastern and a western. The E. section comprises large rooms and two stairways. The rooms are connected by pier-and-door partition. When the doors were open, a series of spacious rooms would be adjoined to form a large space suitable for public gathering (fig. 4, rooms 2-4). Since architecture reflects function, this type of arrangement of interconnec- ted rooms means that the building had a public purpose.

The most important feature of the building is the "Lustral Basin" situated in the most northern part of the E. section of the building within room 3 (fig. 5). A small digression on "Lustral Basins" is necessary to explain their functions in this context.

"Lustral Basins" are small, square rooms with their floors at a level lower than that of the surrounding rooms. They were so named by Sir Arthur Evans who connected them with purification and lustration. Other scholars preferred to call them baths. In fact, these hypotheses are rather arbitrary. It is their superficial similarity with tanks which led Evans, and other scholars, to connect these structures with water and purification. In reality there are no drains attached to any of them neither in Crete nor in Thera. The one in Xeste 3 does not even have a waterproof floor. Sp. Marinatos referred to it as *adyton* (holy of holies) because it seemed to him that this designation might fit the function of this structure better. He was undoubtedly correct because the frescoes surrounding it (fig. 42) depict a goddess and an altar. The *adyton* would be a holy area into which the priests would descend to make offerings, or conduct rituals of a mystical nature. When the doors were shut the priests would be invisible to the public. Let it be noted that the *adyton* was the focal point of the building.

The W. section of Xeste 3 was composed of small rooms, many of which had storage jars and coarse ware (fig. 4a, rooms 6-14). These were the service quarters for storage and possibly preparation of food.

The floor plan of the building was almost identical for both the ground floor and the upper storey. The main difference was that there was no *adyton* on the first storey.

Xeste 3 falls into a category of buildings well attested on Crete. J. Mc Enroe, who made a typology of Minoan houses, found that buildings such as Xeste 3 have large halls with pier-and-door partitions and *adyta* among their characteristics (he calls them house type 1). As in Xeste 3, the storage and industrial units are kept separate from the large rooms. What is important about them is that they reproduce the architectural arrangements of certain quarters of the Minoan palaces. This testifies to their important function and perhaps to their ultimate dependence on the palatial system.

In summary, Xeste 3 was a building with a primarily religious function. The existence of the *adyton* and the fresco with the goddess proves this. It is also evident that there was public participation in the ceremonies as is indicated by the interconnected rooms in the E. section of the building. Undoubtedly people also

5. The adyton ("Lustral Basin").

lived there as well. There was a second storey which may have been used as sleeping quarters; and there were service rooms, the presence of which can be better explained if there were permanent residents in the mansion.

The second type of house consists of a large free-standing building of which the **West House** (fig. 4b) and the **House of the Ladies** (fig. 62) are examples. Although large, these houses do not have ashlar block façades nor rooms connected by pier-and-door partition. Also, they lack *adyta*. An additional difference is that the service rooms are not on the same storey as the large rooms. As a rule service quarters are on the ground floor while ceremonial and residential rooms are on the upper storeys. These differences are due to dissimilarity in function. Before we speculate on what this means, let us observe the similarities. Both types of building have pictorial frescoes. Both have shrines. As has already been noted, the West House had a large window facing the square at which priests may have appeared (fig. 3). Finally, both types of buildings have storage and industrial units. The main difference lies, therefore, in the degree of public function and hierarchy. Xeste 3 was higher in the hierarchy and was constructed to receive people. The West

House, on the other hand, was lower in rank. Its shrine was on the upper floor and was, therefore, inaccessible to the public. The only interaction possible was through a window which we can call "window of appearances" (fig. 3). Buildings such as the West House and House of the Ladies belong to McEnroe's house type 2.

The third type of house can be described as building blocks such as B, Γ, and Δ which are comprised of many rooms. These are connected with some kind of communal living because it is impossible to distinguish individual houses or private dwellings in these blocks. Part of the difficulty is due to the fact that the excavation is not complete in this section and it is impossible to be sure about the communication system of the rooms. But this is not the only reason why we cannot distinguish individual dwellings. Kitchens, which are an indication of the household, have not been found with the frequency one would expect. There seems to be at least one kitchen per block, however, always in the vicinity of a shrine. A hearth and kitchen store-room has been found in sector B (fig. 6), a hearth in the upper storey of Δ, while cooking equipment existed in the Lilies room Δ2 on the ground floor of the same block. The relative scarcity of kitchen arrangements would suggest that each served a small community, or a group of families, rather than one family. On this evidence it appears that some sort of collective organization was operative in the blocks under discussion.

Sector Γ had an industrial character. On the ground floor there were found stone mortars and grinders, stone hammers and other tools. Little remains from the upper floors. The few fresco fragments are non-pictorial.

Before we leave the subject of architecture one more building complex should be considered, the **N. magazines** (fig. 7). It consists of two adjacent buildings separated by a thick double wall which can be distinguished on the left on the plan. The wall forms the W. boundary of the magazines A1-A3 and the E. boundary of the other building which included a mill.

The magazines consisted of three communicating rooms: A1-A3. They had large storage jars arranged on the floor (fig. 9), but there were also smaller vases some of which had a cultic character. In the pithoi there were edible substances such as barley flour, or liquids such as oil, wine and even beer. Some of the pithoi had spouts which leaves no doubt as to their containing liquid.

An interesting architectural feature of rooms A1 and A2 is their large windows facing the street. They were a little above ground level so that they could be used as transaction windows rather than ordinary windows for light. Through the openings distribution and receipt of goods could take place. This is corroborated by the existence of a schist tablet and a small balance found in A2. The former would be used for recording incoming and out going goods, the latter for weighing them.

The existence of cult equipment such as a lion's head rhyton in the magazines (fig. 8), suggests that religious ceremonies took place in the vicinity. It is possible that the place was the square which existed, according to Sp. Marinatos, to the N. of the magazines. The cult equipment may have been handed back and forth through the windows of the store-rooms.

6. Kitchen store-room in sector B.

Room A1 of the magazines included a hearth and cooking pots. We can, thus, infer communal meals for the personnel; it is even possible that cooked food was distributed through the window as a ration payment. It should be noted that corvée labour is well attested in Egypt and the payment was often in terms of rationed food.

The adjacent building to the W. housed a mill which was situated on the ground floor. It is tempting to see a connection between it and the neighbouring magazines: in the former the flour was ground, in the latter it was stored.

7. Plan of the N. magazines of sector A.

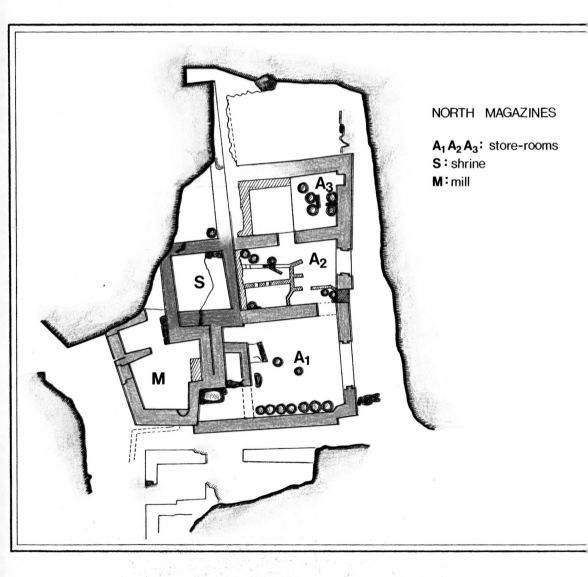

NORTH MAGAZINES

A₁ A₂ A₃ : store-rooms
S : shrine
M : mill

8. Rhyton.

9. Storage jars (pithoi) of the
N. magazines.

On the upper storey of the mill building there existed a shrine (fig. 7). In it were found cult vessels of which the most interesting is a rhyton in the form of a bull covered by a net (fig. 11). The horns are short and blunt, indicating deliberate sawing. It seems that this bull is a representation of a sacrificial animal because the net and the cutting of the horns suggest ritual preparation. It is very probable that sacrificial ritual was connected with harvest of the grain or with its grinding into flour in Crete. If this is so the bull rhyton, seen in connection with the mill, alludes to animal sacrifice.

The mill and the magazines formed a block in the N. part of the settlement. Much has been destroyed in this area but frescoes with religious representations indicate the existence of luxurious apartments as well as shrines on the upper floors. As we have noted, there is evidence of collective operation in the magazines indicated by the existence of the large windows and the distribution or receipt of goods.

11. Bull rhyton found in the shrine close to the N. mill.

12. *Offering table and boar's head rhyton found together in room Δ 17.*

The Shrines

The word shrine has been frequently mentioned in the previous pages. What is shrine and how does one identify it? It is only fair to mention that there is great scepticism among scholars concerning religion. Not all agree that there were any shrines at all at Akrotiri, whereas some would accept only the most obvious ones such as Xeste 3. I have used strict criteria in identifying the shrines and have tried to avoid imposing arbitrary opinions on the evidence.

The criteria for the identification of cult rooms are the following:

1. Existence of frescoes with religious iconography. Let it be noted here that almost all the frescoes of Akrotiri fall into this category as will be argued in the following chapters.

2. Existence of cult equipment such as rhyta (libation vessels), tables of offering, chalices or cups for toasting rituals, etc.

3. Architectural features such as large windows facing squares; or interconnected rooms *(polythyra)*, or simply large spaces where the public could gather.

When these features appear in combination, it is methodologically sound to postulate the existence of a shrine. Using these criteria I have identified seven at Akrotiri which are marked on the plan (fig. 1).

The next question is, "what is a shrine?" The rooms in question are small and could not have accommodated more than a dozen people, in some cases fewer than that. It is, therefore, clear that they were not planned for public worship as the great Temples in the Orient or the large Christian churches. Rather, they were designed to accommodate a few priests only who would conduct offerings on behalf of the community. The public would participate indirectly either by standing in front of the building, in the square, or in rooms within the building which were situated in front of the shrine. Real public gatherings took place in nature, as the evidence from Crete suggests. Peak sanctuaries on mountains, caves or sacred enclosures where such places.

All the shrines at Akrotiri, with the exception of the one near the N. mill, were painted with murals. The significance of the paintings will be examined further on, suffice it to say that the themes were directly related to the type of cult or ritual which took place in the holy room.

The form of the rituals can be inferred by the frescoes and the types of cult equipment. Rhyta and tables of offering are among the most common (figs. 8, 11), but drinking vessels and pitchers also abound because there were apparently toasting rituals connected with the ceremonies. Since we have so many of the objects preserved *in situ* at Akrotiri, we can deduce cultic activities when we find consistent associations between certain vessel types. For example, it is significant when an animal rhyton and a table of offerings are found side by side because this indicates that they were used together: libations were poured on the offering table from the rhyton (fig. 12).

An important activity connected with the shrines involved cult meals. Cooking pots, conical cups (used both as plates and cups), jugs and remnants of meals have been found in almost all the shrines. Sometimes the existence of a hearth near by confirms the hypothesis. This is best illustrated in the case of the shrine B1 (see fig. 1) which had repositories with an offering table, frescoes and a large window facing the square; it therefore has all the characteristics of a cult room. Below B1, a little to the south, there was a kitchen store-room containing many cooking pots and conical cups (fig. 6). Outside this store-room there was a hearth. Thus, food preparation and consumption is attested in the immediate vicinity of the shrine. Another example comes from Δ2, painted with the Lilies fresco (fig. 1); here were found cooking pots and roasting grills. Common meals could take place in front of Δ2, in the large room Δ18 (fig. 1). The shrine of the West House (fig. 16) had a spacious room (6) next to it. In this room were found over one hundred conical cups and pitchers; it was, therefore, a dining room. Finally, there was a room containing cooking pots and conical cups in front of the Room of the Ladies. The latter must have been a shrine

13. Unfinished marble vase from the "House of the Ladies".

not only because of its frescoes but also because there were repositories with cult vessels below its floor and because there was a store-room with ritual vessels adjacent to it (fig. 62, room 7). At Xeste 3 no cooking pots were found but there were small jars, containing remnants of meals, in the rooms in front of the *adyton*. Thus, a picture emerges which consistently associates the shrines with cult meals.

The above should not come as a surprise. In most religions communal meals form an integral part of the cult. Even early Christians ate together after mass to commemorate the Last Supper of Christ.

The seven shrines of Akrotiri are spread widely over the settlement and more will, undoubtedly, come to light in the future. What does their distribution tell us about social organization?

It is noteworthy that there exists only one shrine or shrine - complex per building but that there are more than one in each building block. Thus, block B has two, block Δ has probably two (although the picture is still confused there), etc. Now, we have seen that it is difficult to distinguish between individual dwellings in the blocks. Perhaps the shrines can offer us a clue, however. It is logical that there would be only one shrine per unit; therefore, they can be used as markers of individual units within the building block. Around these shrines are clustered dining areas and/or kitchens, as we have seen. But it was not only meals that were provided because the other types of rooms associated with shrines are industrial sectors or magazines. We have already noted the relationship of the mill and the shrine in two areas:

The mill Δ15 had shrine B1 facing it across the square and the N. mill had a shrine on the upper storey. The N. magazines contained cult vessels along with the pithoi as has already been mentioned. The West House included industrial quarters on the ground floor below its shrines. With the shrine in the House of the Ladies we can perhaps associate a lapidaries' workshop since an unfinished marble vase was found there (fig. 13). There was a storage room below shrine B1 (fig. 14) containing many pithoi embedded in benches. Finally, there seems to have been a mill stone outside the Shrine of the Lilies Δ2. Thus, it is clear that some industrial production or storage was connected with the Akrotiri shrines. A picture emerges which shows the shrines as focal points of the social organization. They serve different functions, both religious and secular. They are most intimately connected with the economy and are agents of social cohesion, since they unite the community in ritual and common meals. Economy and religion are closely connected as is the case also in Minoan Crete. This kind of society might appear strange and implausible to modern readers but it would seem familiar to the contemporaries of the Aegeans in the Ancient Orient. The latter civilizations are better documented than the Minoan, because we have written sources from there and it is a fact that religion played a crucial role in those societies. A short digression on the Mesopotamian temple state might prove useful.

The Mesopotamian Temple State

The land of Sumer of the third millennium B.C. was divided into city states. Each city had at its centre the temple of the deity to whom the city belonged. The temple was not only physically the focus of the city, but it was the centre of all social, commercial and administrative activity. Before the emergence of kings, the city governor, the *ensi*, was the high priest of the temple. He was the representative of the divinity and all his authority emanated from god. The temple was primarily the dwelling of the god. It was also a ceremonial centre, a treasury, a town hall, a store-house, a commercial centre. In addition, it housed the priestly personnel and the temple workers. Thus, it resembled a medieval monastery more than a Greek temple or a Christian church.

A substantial section of the temple was occupied by workshops and magazines (which corresponds exactly to the picture of the so-called palaces in Crete). The reason for this is that the Sumerian economy was controlled by the priesthood to a large extent, although some private enterprise surely existed as well. The function of the temple in the economic system of the Sumerians was to act as a redistribution centre. It amassed wealth from the land it possessed and from tribute. This wealth was then redistributed to the population as wages for their services. Some raw material such as wool or leather would be reworked to a finished product by the temple workers. Stone could be carved to make stone vessels or sculpture. These items would be traded or sent abroad to a foreign king in exchange for other gifts. Corn, oil and fruit could also be exported, but such produce would also be used as payment for the workers. Rations of flour, beer and even clothing were given as wages, as we can tell from the written records of the temples.

14. *Store-room B1 below the shrine of the Antelopes and Boxing Children.*

Regarding the rituals and ceremonies that took place in the precinct of the temple, sacrifices and cult meals were among the most frequent ones. Cult meals are represented on some reliefs from the period.

As we have seen, during some periods the high priest was at the same time the governor of the city. Not only he, but his whole family played an important role in society. There was also a very definite hierarchy in the priesthood. There were higher priests and lower priests, often with very specialized functions. Every person had a fixed position allotted to him by god. Such a system offered stability and a sense of security within its strict and rigid boundaries.

The Akrotiri shrines are much smaller in size and scope than the Mesopotamian temples. There was less centralization and a more egalitarian system of governing. Nevertheless, the Mesopotamian temple organization is illuminating as an analogy and helps us envisage a social system the centre of which was religion.

Priesthood and Nobility

Granted that the shrines are the focal point of religious, economic and social organization, we have to ask the question: who was in charge of them? First of all, it is important to note that the hierarchy among the sanctuaries is reflected in the three types of buildings which have been distinguished; namely, mansions, large independent buildings and building blocks. It is evident that the priests of mansion shrines are hierarchically higher than the priests of smaller shrines such as B1. But who were the priests? Given the great number of sanctuaries, it is difficult to envisage priesthood as an exclusive caste with a very specialized function in society. Rather, it is possible that the priests were members of the noble, ruling class, in fact, they may have been identical with the ruling class. A point in favour of this suggestion is the iconographical representation of priests. In Minoan art it is very difficult to distinguish priestesses from noble ladies since the flounced skirt seems to be the ceremonial costume. There are a few exceptions when a special dress is worn; this is a long robe or skirt made from animal hides (fig. 15). It is possible, however, that these special costumes relate to the particular ritual being performed rather than to status or office. For the above reason, I believe that the priestly class and the nobility were one and the same. Age may have played a role in differentiating and specializing the functions of each priest. Young girls and boys may have been required to spend a period of years in the service of the sanctuary as novices, for example. We shall see later how initiation rituals were celebrated in the context of religious festivities.

The priests, of course, would be in charge of the administration and economy. They would conduct trade and regulate foreign relations. In short, they would be responsible for the welfare of the community and would mediate with the divinity on behalf of the people.

15. The sarcophagus from Hagia Triada.

Relations with Crete

It is evident to the Minoan archaeologist that relations with Crete must have been extremely close since Akrotiri is strongly Minoanized. But what was the nature of this relationship? Some think that the influence of Crete consists only of a cultural veneer which is a common phenomenon when a superior civilization comes into contact with an inferior one. Others see Akrotiri as inhabited by Minoans. My own position is in the middle, between these two extremes. It is difficult to accept that Akrotiri was a Minoan colony because too many of its features are Cycladic. As Ch. Doumas has stressed, there is evidence of continuous habitation on the site from at least the Middle Cycladic period (c. 1800 B.C.). I would also add, that there are features in the cult which are definitely Cycladic, not Minoan. Thus, it does not seem to be true that Akrotiri was inhabited by Minoan colonists only. On the other hand, I cannot accept that the Minoan influence was superficial. It is apparent not only in art, architecture, pottery shapes, script, method of administration (and that is not insignificant), but in the religion as well. The latter shows that this influence was of a profound nature because people do not change their cult patterns without compulsion or proselytism. The adoption of Minoan religion in the 16th century B.C. by the Therans signifies an important event in Cycladic history.

Since religious institutions were in control of the economy at Akrotiri, and since the religion was Minoan, it is possible that the Minoans controlled their outposts through religion. It would be a peaceful but effective way of enforcing Pax Minoica in the Aegean.

The priestly families would have been serving Minoan interests but they need not have been Minoan themselves. What is certain is that both the cult patterns and the economic administration were practiced in a manner similar to that of Crete. A long digression on the similarities between Theran and Cretan religion would be out of place here. The following table shows that the cult patterns were similar because the same cult equipment was used.

Table 1.

Minoan Cult Objects	Present in Thera
Double axes	no
Altars	no
Snake tubes	no
Terracotta feet	no
Tables of offerings	yes
Libation jugs	yes
Rhyta	yes
Conical cups	yes
Shells	yes
Animal-shaped rhyta	yes
Stone offering vessels	yes
Horns of consecration	yes
Red pigment	yes

In addition to the similarity in types of ritual vessels we should note that: (1) The shrine types of Thera and Crete are similar. (2) There is kitchen equipment attested in connection with Minoan shrines. (3) The frescoes of Thera and Crete depict similar themes. Theran religion was, therefore, Minoan.

The Destruction of Akrotiri

The town was destroyed and abandoned in c. 1500 B.C. as a result of an earthquake. This can be deduced from the archaeological evidence since the town already lay in ruins when the eruption of the volcano occurred and buried it under the ashes. The excavations have revealed that houses were standing in ruinous condition when the eruption came. On their ruined walls grass had began to grow. Thus, at least one rainy season had intervened between the earthquake and the eruption.

It was the earthquake which forced the inhabitants to leave. We do not know why this should have happened, since people are usually reluctant to abandon their place of origin and forsake their homes. It is possible that the volcano had given signs of imminent eruption; perhaps the water supply had been destroyed. At any rate, people gathered together their valuables and left. No jewelry or precious metals have been recovered from the site. Only a few bronze vessels and daggers were forgotten. The bulk of finds consist of pottery which is both impractical to carry away and cheap to manufacture.

A few people remained behind and lived a precarious existence in the ruins. Some repairs were undertaken, but the constructions are so provisional that it is hard to see them as part of an organized plan to rebuild the town. Thus, Sp. Marinatos was probably correct in calling them "troglodytes" (dwellers in the ruins).

After some time, probably a few months, the volcano erupted and buried Akrotiri. By this time the squatters must have left since no skeleton has been recovered from the ruins.

In the 1930s Sp. Marinatos formulated a theory which postulated a volcanic destruction of Minoan Crete. He thought that the splendid civilization of that island declined not as a result of earthquakes or invasions, but that it was due to the eruption of the volcano on Thera. He imagined huge *tsunamis* (volcanic waves) which would have hit the coastal sites of Crete, hot ashes falling from the sky and accompanying earthquakes. At that time very few scholars took his theory seriously. When, however, he excavated Akrotiri in the late 1960s, it was thought that his idea had been vindicated and that the site furnished proof of his theory. Recently, opinion has wavered again and it is believed that the difficulties with Marinatos' theory are too serious. The major difficulty has to do with chronology.

The destruction of Crete occurred c. 1450 B.C., namely, fifty years after the abandonment of Akrotiri. These dates are very approximate, however, and it is possible to bridge the gap somewhat. The second difficulty is this: according to volcanologists, the eruption on Thera was not as catastrophic as Sp. Marinatos had envisaged, and would have not affected Crete so severely.

The theory has to be modified in the light of recent research. Yet, I still believe that the insight was basically correct. It is impossible to accept that this eruption did not affect the economy of Crete. The fleet would have been destroyed unless it was at sea. The crops would have been affected as well as the animals. Accompanying earthquakes would have destroyed many buildings. Last, but not least, the eruption would have caused a major psychological crisis. For a people for whom religion was all important, a catastrophe such as this one, regardless of severity, would have meant that the gods were angry. One need only read the Old Testament to visualize how catastrophes are perceived as the wrath of God. The moral blow would have been too hard for Crete to sustain and probably a decline gradually set in. When the Minoan palaces were destroyed in the ensuing years, the Cretans were not able to rebuild them.

17. Reconstruction of room 5 of the West House.

CHAPTER III

The Role of Wall-Paintings in the Bronze Age

"There is hardly a doubt that all human art primarily developed in the service of rituals and that the autonomy of "art for art's sake" was achieved only by another, secondary step of cultural progress." Thus writes K. Lorenz in his book *On Aggression* (p. 73) showing that artistic creation was not only a serious activity but also that it was not devoid of magico-religious connotations.

The question is when this secondary step took place. Had the Minoans already taken this step in the Bronze Age? Most specialists would be prepared to say yes, and they would argue that one function of frescoes was purely decorative. The tone was set by Sir Arthur Evans to whom we owe much of our knowledge and ideas about the Minoans. In a characteristic passage from his *Palace of Minos* II he describes the "House of the Frescoes" at Knossos and the paintings it contained:

> "The house itself was quite a small one... Yet the citizen, we may suppose, of the petty burgher class who had his habitation here is shown by the remains that have come down to us —a mere fraction of the whole— to have been a man of cultivated taste. The painted decoration of the walls is unrivalled of its kind for its picturesque setting, and the many-coloured effect is enhanced, not only by the varied choice of flowers, but the convention of the rocks cut like agates to show their brilliant veins". (pp. 466-67)

Words like "burgher", "cultivated taste", "picturesque" betray Evans' preconceptions: he placed the Minoans in a social setting familiar to that of his own times and hence he described them with a vocabulary which, although perfectly compatible with 19th and 20th century Europe, may be totally inapplicable to a society of the 15th century B.C.

In fact, it is difficult to find purely decorative wall-paintings or sculpture before the end of the Classical period of Greece — if that early. Certainly, large scale art of the early phases of Greek civilization served only two masters: the gods and the *polis*.

But, of course, a better starting point for an investigation of the role of Minoan frescoes is the Bronze Age. Minoan Crete did not exist in a cultural vacuum but was in close contact with the major civilizations of Egypt and the Near East. In both of these, large scale art was used for either of two purposes: expression of religious ideas and practices, or glorification of the ruler. Purely decorative art was at best trivial if it existed at all.

Egyptian tomb paintings had a magico-religious function even if they depicted every day scenes. They were meant to perpetuate the spiritual life of the dead by representing life, in all its manifestations. Temple sculpture had the double purpose of glorifying the god, and the ruler who was himself a living god. In periods of aggression and expansion the Pharaoh was depicted not only as a god but, also, as a conqueror and a victor over forces of chaos. The same is true of Mesopotamia where art revolved around the ruler and his exploits or around the gods.

It can be argued, of course, that very little of private house paintings have survived to either prove or disprove this hypothesis. A few fresco remnants from Amarna (14th century B.C. Egypt) show, however, that the decorative schemes of the houses were not dissimilar to those in the tombs, and there is no doubt that in the latter these were permeated by the religious ideology of the revolutionary king Echnaton. The deceptive naturalism of the Amarna frescoes does not display a "picturesque" or romantic love of nature, they are a tribute to the sun god whose rays sustain life and make it possible in all its forms.

If this is so, then one wonders if Minoan art could be different. Naturally, there were important differences between Crete and the Orient but the similarities were more basic. An Egyptian would not have felt totally alien in Crete, although he would certain feel out of place in the modern world where the values are radically different to his own. Thus, if we are going to approach Minoan mentality at all, and that is all we can do in the absence of written records, we have to see Crete and Thera as part of the larger world of the Ancient Orient. In such a world the words "burgher" or "cultivated taste" would have been meaningless. To quote Henri Frankfort (*Kingship and the Gods,* p. 3) "The purely secular was the purely trivial."

Let us explore the function of Egyptian murals and wall sculpture and the possible analogies with Crete. These functions can be summarized as follows:

1. Propagation of official ideology revolving around the ruler. This is a theme which is either totally absent in Crete and Thera or else thoroughly disguised.

2. Ritual scenes depicting actual ceremonies which are carried out in the very room they decorate. Examples are the sacred barge with the cult image of the divinity which is usually depicted on the walls where the barge was kept in the inner sactuary of Egyptian temples; funeral processions in tombs such as the tomb of Ramose; ceremonial processions beside the stairways of temples, such as the ones in the Hathor temple at Dendera. These types of scenes, where the actual ritual is duplicated on the wall, have close analogies in Grete and, as we shall see, Thera. Suffice it to mention here the tribute bearing procession from the S. corridor of the palace of Knossos which almost certainly reflects the actual ceremony, and the Camp-Stool fresco friezes from the Sanctuary Hall on the *piano nobile* of the same palace.

3. Scenes which are relevant to the function of the space in which they exist but do not reproduce the actual ceremony performed in it. Examples are the offering and festival scenes in the courts of Egyptian temples; funerary and underworld scenes in tombs. Many Cretan frescoes would fall in to this category: the Miniature frescoes of the Grand Stand and Sacred Grove from the palace of Knossos which depict public festivals; the bull-leaping rituals which must have had some connection with the palace, etc.

4. Finally, some depictions enlarge the conceptual and spatial boundaries of the room by means of the representations on the walls. The scenes from every day life in the Egyptian tombs or the nature scenes in Cretan and Theran murals provide an appropriate setting in which the dead or the divinity can transgress the confines of the walls and enter a divine, metaphysical or imaginary sphere. Minoan art like Egyptian art, is thus functional, not decorative.

Does that mean that aesthetics, beautification and decoration were alien to the Minoan people? I would certainly not go so far as to say that. A beautiful work of art is beautiful on its own merits regardless of its function, and there is no doubt that a patron who commissioned a painting would have had certain expectations and aesthetic requirements. Rather, what I am trying to stress is that there was a degree of seriousness in the way the spectator perceived the painting which called for more than the purely decorative. Modern man, contemplating a piece of art in a living room, a museum or a gallery, may derive pleasure or even an emotional experience if the subject moves him. But he remains essentially detached and alien to the work of art. The intentions of the artist remain obscure or may be misunderstood. Besides, modern artists are notorious for refusing to tell the public what they intend. The relationship between art and viewer was very different in the Bronze Age, I believe. For a Minoan or Theran, a painting represented part of his tradition which was comprehensible and even predictable. It can be said that art was a representation of the collective values of the society of which the viewer was a member. Thus, the relationship between art and viewer was intimate and the function of the painting important. As we shall see, the themes centred around religious experiences, although, these could be indirect as well as direct. Political portraiture seems to be totally absent.

In the following chapters I shall try to show the religious associations that lie behind Theran and Minoan frescoes. In fact, Mark Cameron has come to similar conclusions about Cretan frescoes. In the Second Thera Congress he stated: "In my view it was that transference of the cult of a mountain-top goddess to an urban context which inspired the phenomenon of figured scenes and naturalistic pictorial representations in general first in Minoan (and then in other regional fields of Aegean) mural decoration as a fitting means of consecrating the newly erected Second Palaces and their towns to her worship". (*Thera and the Aegean World* II, p. 317).

In summary, Theran paintings have to be studied in their sociological context. Without denying their decorative value, we must go beyond that and ask what they mean and what was the collective experience to which they appealed.

CHAPTER IV

Pictorial Programmes: The West House

In the previous chapter it has been argued that Minoan art was mainly religious in content, and that frescoes had a serious function which went beyond mere aesthetics. If this is so, then it is obvious that the paintings in a room, or a set of rooms, had related themes. Even if each wall or panel had a self-contained subject, it was part of a larger pictorial programme.

What is a "pictorial programme"? The term has been successfully applied by art historians to Roman and later art, and it is especially applicable to Byzantine church paintings. From Roman art, the reliefs on the Ara Pacis Augusti are a good example of a pictorial programme with a distinct political and cultural message. From later times one could cite many examples, among them the Sistine Chapel's paintings by Michelangelo. In all these cases, there is a central idea which is developed successively in various artistic unities.

This approach has seldom been applied to Minoan art. An important contribution was made by L. Morgan who analyzed the West House paintings in relation to each other. R. Hägg applied the term "pictorial programme" to Minoan art in his effort to determine the patron. I am in full agreement with the above scholars and I believe that there is a definite intention behind a group of paintings designed to give a message, or to relate the pictures to the activities which took place in the room.

In reality, it has not been possible to study pictorial programmes in Minoan art prior to the discovery of Akrotiri. The few fresco fragments from Crete were dispersed and knowledge of their exact location on the walls eludes us. Thus, they cannot possibly be studied as coherent groups.

The paintings from the West House will be examined first. They are very well preserved and, what is more, their location on the walls is fairly well documented.

Frescoes existed in rooms 4 and 5 on the upper storey (fig. 16). Offering tables, rhyta and other cult vessels found in these rooms suggest that they formed a shrine complex. As we shall see the iconology or content of the frescoes proves this hypothesis.

It is necessary to describe the plan of the upper floor briefly before the frescoes themselves are discussed (figs. 4 and 16). Rooms 4 and 5 formed a kind of suite, access to which was through a large room 3. Room 6 was a dining hall as can be inferred from the hundreds of conical cups and many jugs found in it. It communicated with the shrine complex (4 and 5) but not with 3. Thus the dining area was an accessory to the shrine. A cupboard, in the corridor between rooms 5 and 6, contained, among other vessels, rhyta and cooking pots. The connection between cult and ritual dining is very well attested in this case.

A visitor entering room 5 from 3 would be surrounded by multiple recesses in the walls of 5 (fig. 17). These recesses would be formed by multiple windows, cupboards and doors. In such a set-up there was very little room left for frescoes and indeed they would hardly have been necessary had their purpose been merely decorative. But there were frescoes. Three sets of friezes were set above the

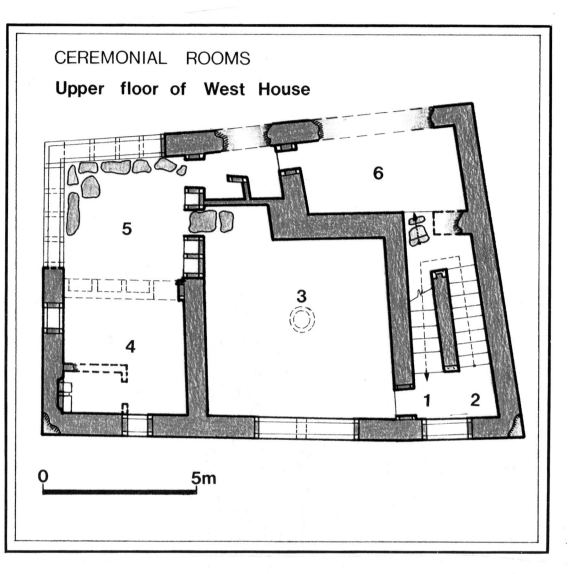

CEREMONIAL ROOMS

Upper floor of West House

5

6

3

4

1   2

0   5m

16. Plan of the West House.

windows, niches or doors of the N., S. and E. walls. The W. wall has yielded no evidence of a frieze. There were also two large panels depicting **nude men carrying fish.** These figures have been called "fishermen" but they cannot be simply that (fig. 18). Two unusual features mark them off as peculiar and indicate that they belong to a group set apart from the rest of the community. These features are their blue heads, which denote partial shaving, and their nudity. The latter should not be confused with heroic nudity of later Greek art. Minoan males are not shown naked unless they are performing a special function as youthful adorants. Granted that the

"fishermen" belong to a special group, what group is it? Shaved heads appear on Egyptian paintings but only on children, and I accept the arguments of Sp. Iakovidis, Ch. Doumas and E. Davis that partial shaving is also used to indicate youth on Theran frescoes. More will be said about this in the following chapter.

Regarding the nudity of the fishermen, we can compare this with nude figures in Minoan art, where the context is always religious. The Kamilari group, where some naked males are making offerings to seated divinities or dead, is one such case. Nude figures exist also in the Metaxas collection, and, most importantly, from Iuktas and from the Dictaean cave.

In view of the above, it can be argued that both the partially shaved heads and the nudity of the two male figures mark them as special persons associated with religion. I believe they are youths making their offering to the deity.

The other important thing about the young adorants is their position in the room. They were placed in the SW. and NE. corners respectively (fig. 17) and they are in a walking position. If they could walk, they would meet in the NW. corner. Could it be that some offering table was placed there to receive offerings such as fish? Indeed, an offering table was found in that corner, resting on the window sill

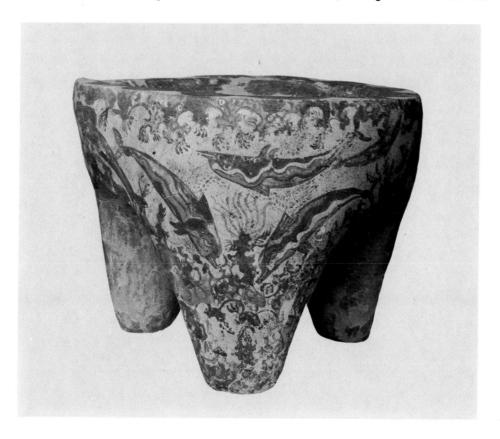

18. *Young adorant carrying fish from room 5, West House.*

19. *Offering table with marine decoration found in room 5 of the West House.*

(fig. 19). It was decorated with dolphins and marine motifs. Thus, the adorants depict an offering that look place in that room, thereby perpetuating it forever. Their function is similar to figures in Egyptians tomb paintings who make offerings to the dead for eternity.

The same room 5 was decorated with friezes set above the windows and cupboards, as has already been noted. They have different subjects which are closely related.

N. Wall Frieze (fig. 20). This is fragmentary but two different scenes are clearly recognizable. I shall start with the one on the right because the painting should be read in this order, as will be argued below. On the lower part there are a few ships, one with a broken bowsprit (lower left corner). The standing man on one ship is dressed in the typical Minoan or Aegean kilt but the drowning men on the lower part of the frieze are naked. This suggests that two different peoples are involved here. On the upper part of the same scene (fig. 21), a coastal settlement is depicted. The men are dressed in tunics and the women in shaggy skirts. They are engaged in normal, everyday activities: women are carrying water from a well, men are bringing the flocks from pasture. A different element is introduced by a row of marching warriors with ox-hide shields and boar's tusk helmets. Their presence has been

20. N. wall frieze depicting a naval engagement in room 5, West House.

21. N. wall frieze, detail.

22. S. wall frieze depicting a naval festival in room 5, West House.

explained in various ways. Some have suggested that they are enemies who have come with the ships and are making an attack on the settlement; others have seen pirates typifying the dangers of the sea. Yet, these interpretations will not do. The warriors, far from attacking the town, seem to be protecting it. The inhabitants appear to be neither afraid nor disturbed by the presence of the armed forces. It seems to me that normalcy can go on be ca use of the warriors, not despite them. If this is so, the warriors are enemies not of the coastal settlement, but of the drowning, naked men. A conflict seems to have taken place, a naval engagement between Aegean warriors and non-Aegean enemies, and the outcome was victory for the Aegeans. The Aegean warriors arrived with their ships to protect the town and they have succeeded. We see the moment of victory when they are marching on the shore in triumph.

Compositionally the scene is very successful. Above, there is order, normalcy; below, there is disorder and defeat. The convention of portraying the defeated enemy naked and in disorder finds very close parallels in Mesopotamian and Egyptian art.

Moving to the left, a quite different scene confronts us. On either side of the crest of a hill stand two groups of men led by their long robed leaders. We have no idea who they are but their clothes might give a clue. The men on the left are wearing kilts like the passenger on the Aegean ship. The men to the right, on the other hand, are wearing tunics similar to those of the inhabitants of the coastal settlement. It is therefore reasonable to postulate that the two peoples involved are the Aegeans (Therans?) who have arrived with their ships and the inhabitants of the town which was under attack. The gestures are formal and the occasion appears to be a solemn one. This has led Sp. Marinatos and other scholars to the conclusion that a ceremony of a religious nature is taking place. I suggest that it is a thanksgiving ceremony for the victory. In summary, the N. wall frieze depicts the victory of Aegeans (Therans?) over their non-Aegean enemy.

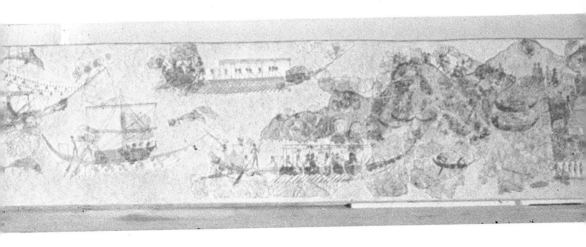

The S. Wall Frieze (fig. 22) was situated on the opposite wall. Some features, like the warriors, recur here which has led scholars to think that the two friezes should be read as a sequel. Although this is not correct, as we shall see, it is certain that the two were related. The S. frieze depicts a procession of ships, splendidly adorned, which moves between two towns. The left (E.) one is clearly more simple than the right (W.) one which is also the culminating point of the journey. It has been recognized that the right town is Akrotiri itself. But where is the fleet coming from? Sp. Marinatos postulated an expedition to Libya from which the ships are returning. Yet, this is difficult to accept. As has been shown by P. Warren, the topographical elements on the fresco are completely compatible with an Aegean setting and the same can be said about the flora and the fauna. The method used for the propulsion of the ships, paddling, cannot have been applied during a long journey. Last, but not least, the special ornamentation of the ships with nature symbols, such as flowers, butterflies and swallows, betokens a religious occasion, not a homecoming from a military expedition. The subject of the frieze is a festival, where the fleet plays an important role.

More will be said about the nature of the festival in the next chapter. For the moment some details are worth observing. The two towns on the left and right ends of the ship fresco (S. wall) are rendered differently. The left town (fig. 23) has simple buildings. In its outskirts we see some rustics, dressed in animal hides, who are conversing across a river. In the town, people are watching the fleet standing either on the roofs of the houses or on the shore line. They are dressed in tunics, not kilts or long robes. Thus, it seems that tunics indicate a type of dress worn by provincials or the common town's people. The town in question may be a dependency of Akrotiri, either on Thera itself or on a neighbouring island. That the landscape above the town has a symbolic, rather than a topographical significance will be argued later. Here, let it only be said that it is unlikely that lions roamed on the dry Aegean islands.

23. S. wall frieze, left town.

The ships vary in size. The passengers are wearing either tunics or long robes. It is reasonable to suggest that they represent people of higher status. This is all the more likely because the ships are in parade and a display of status is surely involved.

The right town (fig. 24) is, in all probability, Akrotiri, as we have noted. There is little doubt that it is more sophisticated than the one previously described and than the coastal settlement depicted on the N. wall. The building complexes are impressive and there are horns of consecration to the right of the gate; these horns are emblems of religious authority (see ch. II). The inhabitants represent both sexes, all ages and social strata. Rustics are designated by their shaggy skin dresses, they are visible on the left edge of the town on the upper part of the frieze. Men with tunics, the common town's people, are shown on the upper part of the frieze above the buildings

24. S. wall frieze, right town, probably Akrotiri.

Another category of people are watching from the windows and balconies. They consist of women, who are in prominent positions on the balconies, men and at least one child. The latter is behind the priestess on the balcony with horns of consecration (fig. 24). These figures probably represent the nobility.

Men running to and fro from the town to a watch-tower situated high upon a cliff appear to be youthful. They are either naked or wearing only loincloths. The same can be said about the attire of a fisherman carrying a pole from which are suspended baskets or nets. He is moving from the shore towards the town.

There is a formal procession of youths, moving past the city gate towards the harbour, leading an animal for sacrifice. On the few figures where the dress is discernible, it is clear that they are wearing kilts. Thus, the kilt seems to be worn on special (ceremonial?) occasions. The following table summarizes the observations on social divisions and dress.

25. E. wall frieze depicting hunting in a river landscape in room 5, West House.

Table 2

Tunics	Common townspeople and provincials (compare with N. wall frieze).
Kilts	Young persons of high social standing (people in the ships) or taking part in a procession (procession of youths).
Shaggy Animal Hide Dress	Rustics
Long Robes	Adults who are nobles, leaders or priests.
Naked Men	Youths not initiated yet (compare with Egyptian conventions of the New Kingdom).

The evidence is important for the Theran society of the 16th century B.C. and it reflects also the situation in Crete where similar observations can be made about the dress. However, I think it is more valid as an insight into the mentality of the period, than as an accurate, realistic picture. I doubt that rustics always wore animal hide dresses and provincials or commoners always tunics. But the artist of the S. wall frieze intended to give as representative a picture of the whole society as possible. In this way he managed to show the total participation of the town in the festival.

The E. Wall Frieze (fig. 25) depicts a river landscape with palms and papyri. Two predatory animals, a wild cat and a griffin, chase their prey, a bird and a deer respectively.

This painting is autonomous, which explains why it has different dimensions, being slightly narrower than the N. and S. wall friezes. Yet, it is thematically related to them by the theme of aggression. If victory and warriors are present on the other frescoes, here the relationship of predator to prey suggests the same thing. More will be said about that further on (ch. V).

Seeing the friezes as independent but thematically related units is an important step towards understanding the pictorial programme and the idea behind it. In this case the dominant ideas are victory and festive celebration. The naked, young adorants on the panels of the same room (fig. 18) fit with the same general theme since they are males offering fish which connects them with the marine festival and the fleet.

26. *Priestess from the door leading from room 4 to room 5, West House.*

27. *Priestly figure (after Evans, PM IV, fig. 336).*

Yet another large panel could be associated with room 5, the **"young priestess"** (fig. 26). This painting was thought to have been placed in the next room (4) by Sp. Marinatos, but Ch. Doumas has argued that it decorated the door which led from 4 to 5. If this is correct, then the priestess is represented as walking from room 4 to 5.

She has a hairstyle which is very unusual. If the blue colour of the head denotes partial shaving, then the lock on top of the head is dressed in such a way as to resemble a snake. This is not common for either male or female shaved youths at Akrotiri. She also has peculiar body paint. Not only are the lips painted a very vivid red (which is not common even in Crete), but her ear is painted red as well. Red ears are attested on a fresco fragment from Pylos, but unfortunately we have no context for it. There is also a figurine with a red ear from Malia.

Also her costume is unusual for a female since the usual ceremonial dress involves a skirt, very often a flounced one. This figure, however, wears a blue blouse, decorated with a white starry pattern, and over it a yellow robe which is shaggy and may imitate skin. It is a kind of "sari" worn over the blouse.

A good parallel for such a dress can be seen on a seal representation depicting a figure holding a bird (fig. 27). The man is identified as a priest. In both cases the dress goes over the shoulder and indicates a special ceremonial garment not to be equated with any long dress. It is noteworthy that Egyptian priests were also distinguished by the strip of linen passing over one shoulder and this strengthens the suspicion that this type of attire was worn by officiating priests or priestesses.

Other parallels, also from seals, depict the same costume on male persons of apparently priestly status to judge from the symbols of authority which they hold. Note especially the man accompanied by a griffin who has been called by Evans a sacerdotal figure (fig. 27). The characteristic feature of this costume, as already noted above, is the length of the robe and the arrangement of part of it over the shoulder. Perhaps the priestess from the West House is the first example of a professional that we have on a fresco from Thera. There is no doubt that she is differentiated from other females by her unusual hairstyle, costume and body paint and it is significant that she is not wearing the festive flounced costume which is ordinarily worn by women. The object she holds in her left hand looks like an incense burner on which coals are glowing. On these she is sprinkling a yellow substance (saffron?) which would produce a fragrance when burned. Thus, not only her costume but the object she is holding identify her as a priestess.

Room 4 was decorated with some eight paintings (fig. 28) of certain objects which have been identified as the cabins which we see on the ships of the S. frieze (fig. 22). They consist of wooden poles wrapped by ox-hide and ending in waz-lilies, an Egyptian religious symbol. The cabins were placed on the back of the ship, therefore they have probably a ceremonial significance. On Egyptian ships the captain's cabin was normally placed in the front so that he could have a good view ahead of him whereas the ceremonial cabin of the king or queen was placed in the middle. The cabins then allude to the marine festival which is depicted on the S. frieze and with which the West House was connected. It is even possible to interpret them as emblems of the religious leader of the largest ship (fig. 36).

28. Panel representing the captain's cabin, room 4, West House.

Some additional points further elucidate the nature of these murals. The actual cabins on the ships were probably movable and that is why the term "palanquin" could also be used to describe them. They could be placed on or off the ships as Ch. Doumas and L. Morgan have argued. This would suggest a ceremonial usage which is supported also by the evidence from seals where these cabins appear alone, possibly as emblems. It is clear, therefore, that they had some intrinsic importance.

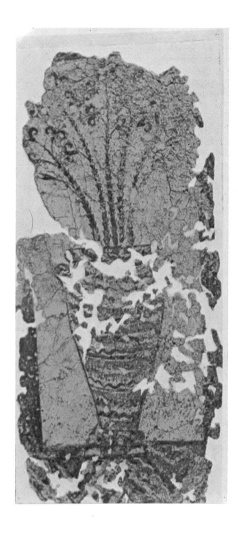

29. Lilies in flowerpots. From the window-jambs of room 4, West House.

The last paintings from the West House which will be discussed depicted **lilies growing in flowerpots** (fig. 29). They decorated the jambs of a window in room 4. It is not without significance that the flowers are in pots, not growing out of doors. The reason behind this choice is that the flowers are decorative here, alluding to real flowerpots which would have been placed on the window sill during festive occasions which must have taken place in the spring when lilies bloom. Landscapes, on the other hand, have a different function (see ch. VI) which would be out of place in this programme. Thus, the lilies perpetuate a festive decoration, just as the humans perpetuate a ritual.

I have argued above that room 5 was the main shrine but what about 4? The architecture and the finds suggest that it was a preparatory room. There was a bath-tub and a bronze cauldron in the corner 4a which must have been used in connection with water (fig. 16). A bench with a slit in the middle was connected to a drain pipe that run vertically down the outside wall. This indicates that water or liquids were poured down there (fig. 30). A table of offerings and a lion's head rhyton,

30. Bench with a slit in the middle which is connected by a vertical
pipe to a drainage system; room 4, West House.

as well as cups, were among the finds which suggest offerings. Finally, there was a
broken bowl containing red pigment which I think was used on the "priestess" as
body paint. As we have seen, the latter had not only vivid red lips but a red ear as
well.

In view of the above, it is arguable that room 4 was used for preparation involving
offerings and purification with water and painting of parts of the face in red. It will be
remembered that the painting of the "priestess" was found exactly on the door jamb
leading from 4 to 5 as though she is passing from one room to another.

In summary, the pictorial programme includes two kinds of frescoes: the friezes
and the large panels. Whereas the former have more of a narrative content and
relate to the festival, the latter perpetuate an actuality which was connected with the
room. The adorants conduct an offering ritual, the "priestess" is holding her incense
burner, and the flower pots decorate the room. By painting these scenes the
Akrotirians made the power of the ritual effective for ever.

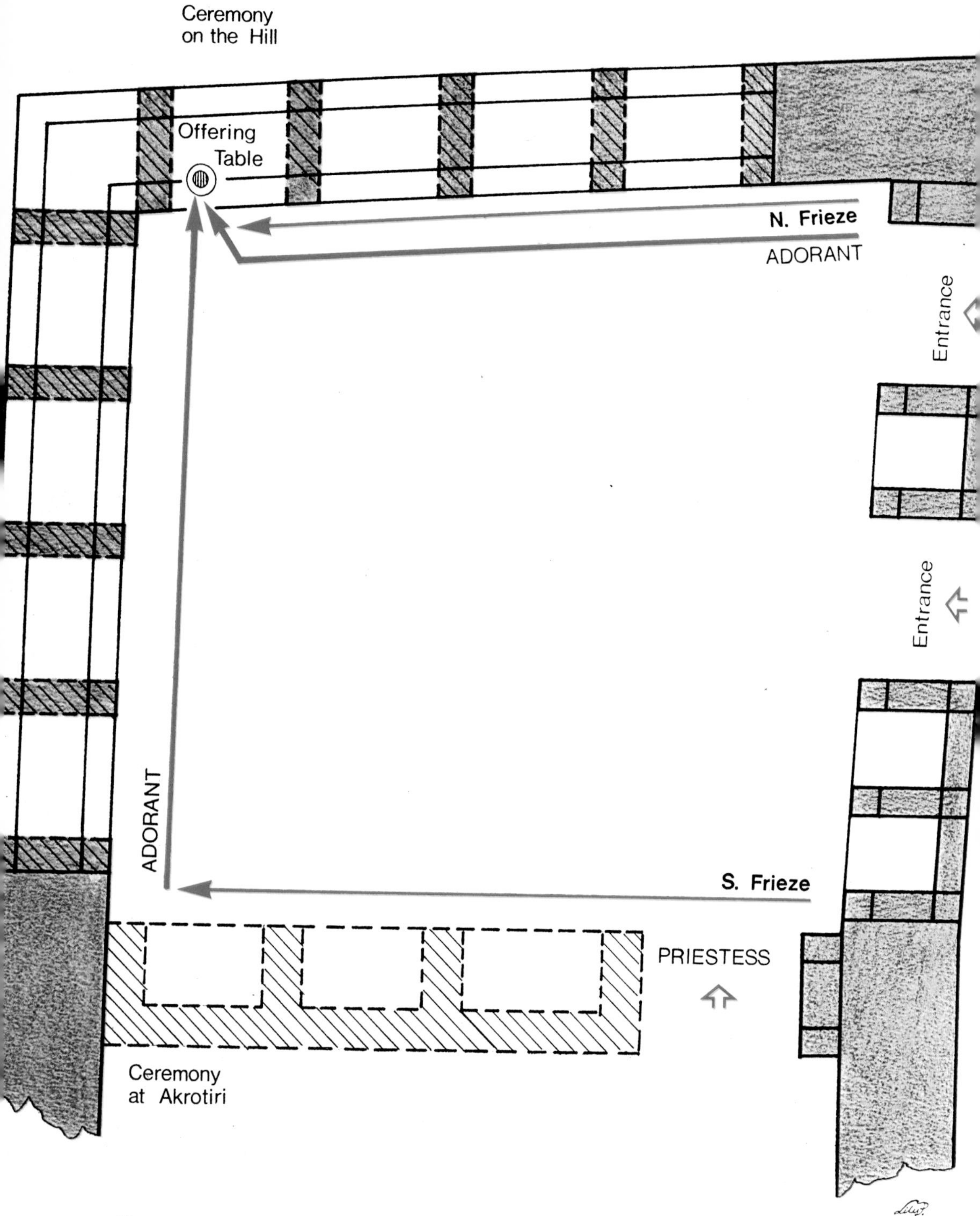

Ceremony
on the Hill

Offering
Table

N. Frieze

ADORANT

Entrance

Entrance

ADORANT

S. Frieze

PRIESTESS

Ceremony
at Akrotiri

Another question which should be discussed involves how to read the friezes. Should one go around the room and read first the N. wall then the S. one and finally the E. wall? Or should it be the other way around? Again it seems to me that the whole pictorial set up should be considered before we reach a final answer. The young adorants carrying fish can be used as "sign posts", a term M. Cameron has used for some Knossian frescoes. Since the adorant of the NE corner is moving in an E. - W. direction, I do think that the frieze also should be read that way (fig. 31). Consequently, the first alternative should be excluded. On the other hand the S. wall frieze could not be read from W. to E. because the culminating point of the narrative lies in the W. corner where the town of Akrotiri is depicted. Thus, the second alternative must be excluded as well. In short it appears that the N. and S. wall friezes should be read in a parallel fashion from E. to W., as one would move from the entrance of room 5 towards the W. wall (fig. 31).

I have suggested before that something important was taking place in the W. of the shrine, especially the NW. corner where the adorants would meet, had they been able to walk. An offering table found there strengthens this suspicion. Now, if we add the evidence deduced from the method of reading the friezes, the suspicion becomes almost a certainty. The S. frieze ends in the town of Akrotiri where a festive celebration is conducted. The N. one ends in a ceremony on the hill which I suggested was thanksgiving for victory. Thus the W. end of both frescoes ends in religious ceremonies.

The above indicates that the pictorial programme was carefully planned and thought out before it was put into effect. From the artistic point of view several hands are discernible (the "priestess" is a little more crudely painted than the adorants) and it is certain that several painters were at work. Who planned this operation? Perhaps it was the priestly family residing in the West House who was in charge of running the festival.

A final issue has to be tackled and that is the question of public participation. Since the festival was public, the main celebration took place in the open and, especially by the harbour. In the West House only some of the rituals, perhaps of a preparatory nature, would be performed, conducted by a few priests. This explains why the shrine was on the upper floor and was not easily accessible. However, there was a large square in front of the West House and perhaps another behind it. A lot of people could be accommodated there and could participate indirectly in the ritual. The multiple window arrangement of the main shrine 5 is certainly not accidental and would allow a partial view of the action. I would also suggest that the procession may have started from the square in front of the West House (fig. 3) which still impresses the visitor with its monumentality and its large window of appearances.

31. Plan showing how the friezes should be read in room 5, West House.

CHAPTER V

Public Festivals on Theran Fescoes

One of the most important aspects of organized religion is public festivals. They serve a variety of functions which operate both on the psychological and social level. They provide entertainment, they promote unity and social cohesion, and they allow a legitimate outlet for emotions.

The organization of the festivals often mirrors the social hierarchy and role division of the community. In this way the traditional roles are reinforced and reaffirmed. Not only that, new roles are created for the youths who are making the transition from childhood into adulthood to be prepared for their new responsibilities as fully integrated members of the society.

In Classical Greece there were festivals where only women could participate, the men being excluded. Examples are the Thesmophoria as well as some Dionysiac festivals. On the other hand, there were many exclusively male festivals where contests were performed, such as the *Gymnopaideia* in Sparta. There were also processions such as the *Septeria* at Delphi celebrated in connection with Apollo. Finally, in festivals such as the Panathenaia the whole community participated in their distinctive roles. Male youths took part as competitors in the chariot races, mature men as hoplites, virgins as carriers of the baskets and the peplos of the goddess, etc. Thus, role division and hierarchy were reinforced.

The seasonal dimension of festivals should not be neglected either, since many, if not all, public celebrations in antiquity were intimately connected with nature.

In Egypt and Mesopotamia, in cultures contemporary with Minoan Crete, festivals played a crucial role, reflecting the relation between society and nature. According to Henri Frankfort: "Mesopotamian society was entirely adapted to the cyclic succession of the seasons... Society moved in harmony with nature through a recurring sequence of religious festivals. In celebrating them, the human community participated actively in the cosmic crises which the seasonal changes represented..." (*Kingship and the Gods,* p. 3).

In Egypt, too, the rhythm of the seasons was reflected in the calendar of the official year. There were annual festivals connected with the rise of the Nile and the completion of the harvest.

It is important to note in this context that before natural sciences and meteorology enabled man to predict seasonal phenomena, the changes in nature were perceived as crises similar to social changes. Society was endangered since its survival depended on the outcome of the harvest and it had to harmonize itself with nature.

We shall now look at Theran festivals as they are represented on the frescoes and we shall note how the aspects which have been touched upon above are reflected in the art.

The first fresco I shall discuss is the Miniature friezes from the West House room 5, which depict a marine festival. The friezes were set above windows or recesses in the walls, which served as cupboards, and the covered three out of the four walls of the room (fig. 17). Thus, only the W. wall has yielded no evidence of a frieze which, had it existed at all, has left no fragments.

The interpretation of these friezes has been the subject of much controversy and various theories have been proposed. Summarized briefly these theories are: military expedition involving Mycenaeans; expedition to Libya; shipwreck typifying the dangers of the sea, etc.

It has been also suggested that a religious scene is represented here, a view with which I agree. My own interpretation has already been presented in the previous chapter. Here I shall merely emphasize the main points and make some additional ones because the interpretation of these friezes bears directly on the subject of Theran festivals.

My belief is that a religious festival and not an expedition of some kind is depicted. This can be deduced from the following details: 1. The special ornamentation of the ships of the S. wall frieze which betoken a festive occasion. 2. A woman of obviously great status is standing on a balcony in the right town of the S. wall frieze. Next to her are visible horns of consecration which define her function as a priestly one (fig. 32).

32. Woman standing on a balcony with horns of consecration.
Detail from S. wall frieze, room 5, West House.

3. The ships of the same frieze are paddled, not rowed. This is an impractical and archaic method of propulsion which can be explained only if it is carried out in a ritual context but not if the ships came from a distant expedition. 4. On the same frieze there is a procession of youths in the right town, who are leading an animal for sacrifice and that is a religious act (fig. 33).

These four points show that the ships and the right town (which I believe is Akrotiri) are taking part in a festive occasion. In other words, a marine festival is depicted as L. Morgan has also argued.

Let us now try to define this festival a little more closely. So far I have stressed the religious element. There is, however, another important element which has to be taken into account: a military one. Most of the ships have helmets hanging from the cabins or the awning above the passengers (fig. 35). In addition spears are visible next to the cabins. This is obvious military equipment. Aggression is represented in a symbolic fashion also, since most of the ships have lions or griffins at their sterns. The former are, of course, the predatory animals *par excellence*. Hunting lions appear also as emblems on the sides of the largest ship (fig. 34). The lion chasing his prey is a very appropriate image invoking military aggression. Now, the artist has given extra emphasis to this concept by adding a lion chasing deer on the landscape scene on the left side of the frieze. I suggest that this is not a superfluous landscape element for decorative effect but a meaningful image which reinforces the idea of aggression. In this way the latter is shown on two levels; a social and a natural one.

33. Procession of youths leading an animal to sacrifice.
Detail from S. Frieze, room 5, West House.

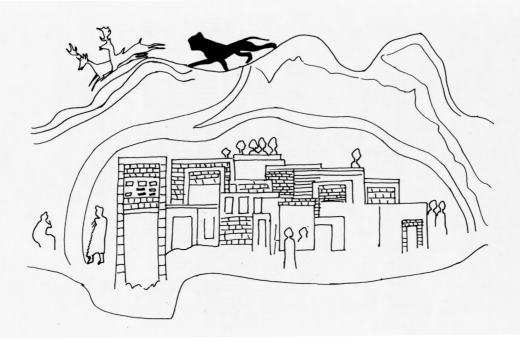

34. Simplified drawing showing the motif of chasing lions on the ships and in the landscape of the S. frieze, room 5, West House (drawing by D. Georgiou).

35. Drawing of the best preserved ship of the fleet from the S. frieze, room 5, West House (after Thera VI, fig. 5).

Let us now look at the frieze of the E. wall (fig. 25). On the surface it looks unrelated to the ship fresco, but on closer inspection the theme of aggression appears again as the main subject. Two predators, a griffin and a wild cat, are chasing their prey near a river. Thus, this frieze is thematically related to the ship fresco, although it is autonomous.

It remains to consider the N. wall frieze (fig. 20) and to see how this is related to the marine and military festival. Although this fresco is incomplete, enough is preserved for us to understand the main theme. As we have already seen in the previous chapter, it depicts a sea battle between Aegeans and their enemies. Aegean warriors are recognizable by their characteristic military equipment. The alien enemy is identifiable by the non-Aegean shields and nudity which is a convention for defeat in Egyptian and Mesopotamian art. Note the grappling-iron which shows that a naval engagement has taken place. This is important because it excludes the shipwreck hypothesis.

The outcome of the naval engagement is clear. The enemy is drowning, whereas the Aegean warriors are marching victoriously on land. Life in the coastal village can go on as normal because the threat has been nullified. In short, the N. wall frieze depicts an Aegean victory over alien enemies. The orderly life of the village has been re-established.

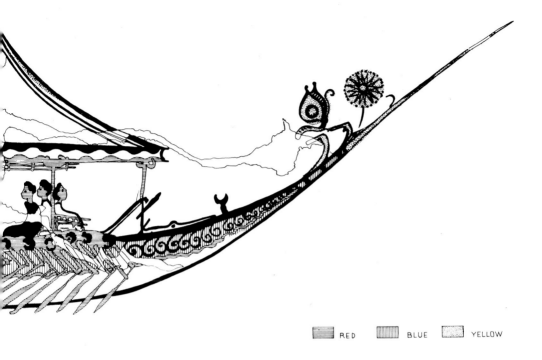

Now, if we look at the three walls as a complex of autonomous but related pictorial messages (fig. 17), an interpretation does emerge. The N. wall depicts a realistic event. (Here I should stress that I do not believe that these people had a sense of history similar to our own.) This event refers to a victory of the Aegeans over their enemies. The S. wall depicts a recurring festival which celebrates this victory, and in which the fleet is the protagonist, although the whole populace participates. It is a marine festival insofar as it involves the fleet. It is a military one insofar as it involves victory. The E. wall depicts aggression in nature.

Let us now focus on the central topic of this chapter, namely, how the festival in question reflects social hierarchy and role division and how it is related to seasonal cycles.

Hierarchy is evident, firstly, among the ships and, secondly, among the passengers of the ships (fig. 21). The size of the former varies as well as the degree of ornamentation. The smaller boats have hardly any ornaments and no cabin with a captain. Especially interesting is the hierarchy among the passengers (fig. 35). The captain is always seated in a cabin or palanquin which is set apart, in the stern of the ship. Close to the captain are two to four more persons, some seated, some standing. While the standing men could be helmsmen, the seated ones, usually facing each other, can be interpreted as attendants of the captain. They are persons

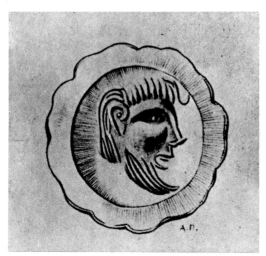

36. Close-up of the "leader" in the largest sh. Note the lilies crowning his cabin; S. frieze, room 5, West House.

37. Amethyst seal from Mycenae, probably showing a Minoan priest.

of a certain social standing and their position near the captain alludes to their special status. In the smaller boats such attendants are lacking.

Clothing also indicates hierarchy, age, or at least specialized function. The standing persons, wearing kilts, seem to be performing a job, whereas the seated passengers, including those under the awning, are wearing long robes. Finally, the beard of the leader, seated in the largest ship, should not be overlooked (fig. 36). It is likely that only persons of high rank had beards as can be inferred from portraits on seals (fig. 37).

Not only is hierarchy evident on the ship fresco but role division as well. The latter is very striking indeed. The festival in question is clearly one where males are the protagonists. Women do, in fact, appear in prominent places on the balconies but they are passive participants only (fig. 24). There are no women on the ships, nor is there any in the procession which is moving past the city gate towards the harbour.

We turn now to the procession (fig. 38). All the members are young males wearing kilts. As mentioned above, this is a religious procession as can be inferred by the animal which is led for sacrifice, and, also, by the ritual gestures which recall the Harvesters' procession on the vase from Hagia Triada (fig. 39). If these are indeed youths, then we have here an example of new role creation which is often a characteristic of public festivals. The youths are the warriors of tomorrow. In this festival they are admitted into manhood and their new role is defined. This suggestion finds support in the following observations. Firstly, among the passive participants watching from the balconies or roof terraces are children and men (fig. 24). The men I take to be adults who do not have sufficient status to be on the ships but who are past the age of initiation. Secondly, in the same room 5 where the friezes were found, there existed two large panels depicting young, naked men usually referred to as "fishermen" (fig. 18). In the previous chapter I have expressed the view that they are in fact adorants offering fish to the deity and I have based this on their hairstyle, nudity, and position in the room. Here it is important to note that they are young males and I agree with those who have connected the partial shaving of the head with initiation and youth. We shall see that this holds true for young females as well. Thus, the youths offering fish are depicted in the room because of their special role in the festival. The fish are appropriate as offerings since the festival is a marine one.

Regarding the so called priestess, we have seen that she is wearing a special costume, and it will be remembered that this costume type is worn by males of apparently priestly status.

So far the following points have been established about the festival in question. 1. It celebrates a victory over a non-Aegean enemy. 2. It is a celebration where males are the protagonists. 3. The existing hierarchy and role division of society are reinforced. Although all members of the community are participating, they do so in their distinctive roles. 4. There is creation of new roles.

The final issue I shall touch upon in connection with these frescoes involves the problem of seasonal cycles. It has been observed by L. Morgan that a number of elements on the ship fresco allude to the spring/early summer. Some of these

38. *Procession of youths from S. wall frieze, room 5, West House.*

elements are the emblems on the ships (fig. 3). A butterfly and flower on the bowsprit on the last ship to the left (upper register); a swallow and flower on the bowsprit of the last ship to the left (lower register).

Many of the emblems are concentrated on the largest ships there are; butterflies on the bowsprit, lilies on top of the cabin poles and flower festoons hanging from the mast. Finally, there were paintings of lilies in flowerpots decorating the window jambs of room 4 in the West House (fig. 29). All these motifs are hardly accidental and, when seen together, they suggest that the festival took place in the spring. But can it be both a seasonal and victory festival? Does not the interpretation previously suggested that a victory is celebrated exclude such a possibility? I would like to suggest that, far from being mutually exclusive, the ideas of victory on the one hand, and of the coming of the spring on the other, were closely connected in the E. Mediterranean mentality of that period. This is because victory on the human level acquires an added significance when it is realized in the victory of nature over the period of winter barrenness. For the mythopoeic mind, nature is also struggling to overcome hostile forces and its reawakening in the spring is a victory. To use an analogy, it is not an accident that in the Babylonian New Year Festival, Marduk's victory over the forces of chaos was realized in nature by the coming of spring. Nor

39. Harvesters' vase from Hagia Triada. Compare the gestures of the men with those of fig. 38.

is it an accident that in Christianity the triumph of Christ over death at Easter occurs in the spring. Thus, the real date and circumstances of the victory of the Aegeans does not matter. The event acquires its meaning when it is manifested in the eternal, unchanging and recurring natural forces which integrate it in the cosmic order.

The next fresco, or rather groups of frescoes, which will be discussed come from Xeste 3, one of the most important buildings of Akrotiri so far excavated. The focal point of this building was an *adyton,* which has been described in chapter II (fig. 5). It is clear that this was a sacred area designated for some special ritual, perhaps of a mystical nature. Above the *adyton* were two frescoes corresponding to the ground floor level and upper storey respectively. A sketch shows the composition, which is now in the final stages of restoration in the laboratories.

On the upper storey the subject of the composition is crocus gathering (fig. 40). Women are picking the flowers in a rocky landscape and place them in baskets. Dominating the scene is a female figure seated on a tripartite platform and flanked by two exotic animals, a monkey and a griffin. That this figure is a goddess is certain. She is physically separated from the human community by the platform, the tripartite form of which has definite religious connotations; also it is resting on incurved altars.

The goddess is symbolically separated because her animal attendants are exotic and one is fabulous; we are thus in the realm of the fantastic. The meaning of this fresco is clear. Women dressed in festive clothes and wearing expensive jewelry are picking crocuses and are offering them to the goddess. What kind of occasion is this? From the clothes and jewelry that the women wear, we can deduce that this is a festival, the exact significance of which will become clear after we have analyzed the scene further.

One point which deserves special attention is the age group of the women. They have either short, curly hair with a pony tail (fig. 41), or a shaved head with only a pony tail and a forelock (fig. 42). It has been observed by Ch. Doumas, E. Davis and Sp. Iakovidis independently that partial shaving of the hair is an indication of youth. Indeed, this is closely paralleled in Egypt. We have already seen examples of partially shaved males in the case of the adorants from the West House (fig. 18). Here we have the female counterpart. On the Crocus Gatherers fresco the two stages of hair growth are represented very clearly. Some girls have shaved heads while others have short curls which are just growing out of the scalp.

The hypothesis of the youth of the girls is also strengthened by the following observation: none of the crocus gatherers has prominent breasts.

The fresco below the Crocus Gatherers was directly above the *adyton* and was visible from the ground floor only (fig. 43). Three girls are depicted, the central one of which is wounded in the foot. Only one has a shaved head but the other two are also young since they have long hair. As we shall see, older women have their hair bound up in a bun. I am grateful to Ellen Davis for this observation.

The significance of the wound will be dealt with in the next chapter. Suffice it to say here that the *adyton* fresco depicts a ritual where young girls are the protagonists.

0. Sketch of the fresco of the Crocus Gatherers; and E. Walls, room 3, Xeste 3.

1. Girl with curly hair; E. all, upper floor, room 3, este 3.

2. Girl with shaved head; . wall, upper floor, oom 3. Xeste 3.

43. Sketch of the adyton fresco, S. wall, ground floor, room 3, Xeste 3.

Seeing the two frescoes of the *adyton* as a unit, it is reasonable to suggest that we are dealing with a festival where the main actors are female, specifically young girls. Inevitably one thinks of initiation and creation of new roles which I have postulated for the youths the marine festival from the West House. The young girls may be initiated into their new roles as wives and mothers. We have seen that in such festivals members of the community other than the initiates partake. The frescoes which have just been discussed depict young girls only but if we look at the whole pictorial programme of the room, we shall see that males and older women feature as well, but only as marginal participants (fig. 44).

At least four male figures were painted on the W. wall of the groundfloor of room 3, the room of the *adyton*. Some have shaved heads and are naked; they are, therefore, young. The others have normal hair and wear kilts, they are thus probably adults. The males are carrying objects, possibly as offerings to the *adyton.* They are, thus, connected with the ritual scene of the *adyton* but they are not included in the *adyton* fresco itself because they are marginal participants.

Three female figures were painted probably on the S. wall of the same room but on the upper floor, corresponding to the level of the Crocus Gatherers (fig. 44). Two torsos of these women have been published by Sp. Marinatos in *Thera* VII. One is carrying a bunch of flowers which appear to be wild roses *(cistus)* (fig. 5). Both have costumes on which real flowers are embroidered: crocuses in one case (fig. 46) and lilies (fig. 45) in the other. It is important to note the hairstyles in this context. Both have hair bound at the nape of the neck. This indicates that this group was

composed of older, mature women. The latter observation is supported by the fact that one of the women has very large breasts.

Thus, if we look at the pictorial programme (fig. 44) of both floors of room 3, it is clear that both sexes and all ages are represented. Still, only the young girls have a prominent position and they are clearly the protagonists of this festival.

Let us now see how this festival is connected with nature. In the frescoes from Xeste 3 flowers, plants and even animals feature so prominently, that no theory about the significance of the frescoes can be satisfactory without taking them into consideration.

Foremost among the flowers are the crocuses. Not only do they appear on the *adyton* frescoes but also on the costumes of two women as well as on a frieze from the neighbouring room 2. Given the prominence of the crocus on the fresco programme, and given the fact that young girls are picking them, it is tempting to make a connection. It has, therefore, been suggested that the crocus has some connection with initiation. Indeed saffron can be used as a drug and is considered a pain killer during menstruation. Saffron is also a valuable substance for food flavouring and dyeing fabric. I would by no means deny the importance of saffron for industrial and medicinal purposes. However, I feel that the significance of this flower lies elsewhere in this particular context. Let us observe first that the saffron crocus grows in the late autumn. Yet, the predominant symbolism in the frescoes from Xeste 3 alludes to the spring. Crocuses coupled with swallows are depicted on a frieze from room 2 (fig. 47), as well as on a "strainer" found in room 3 (fig. 48). It is

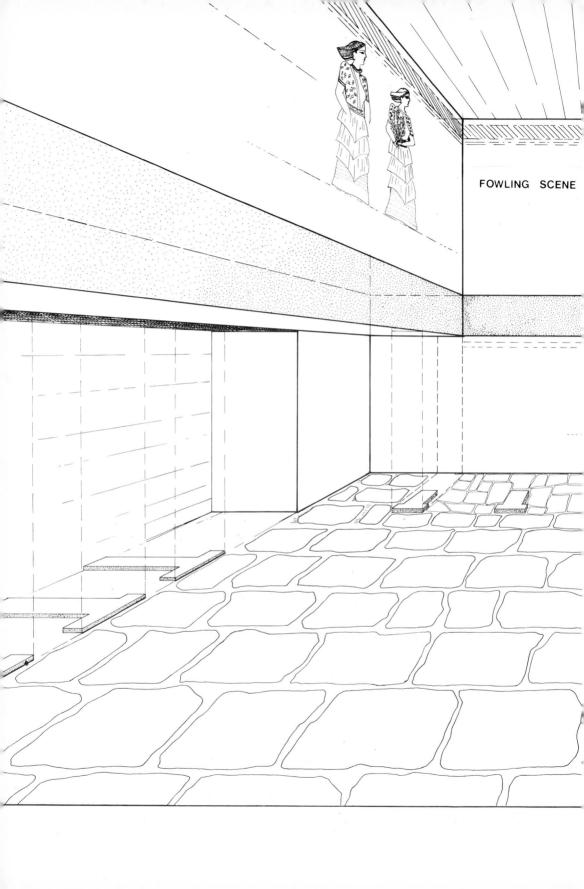

FOWLING SCENE

44. Tentative reconstruction of the entire room 3 showing the pictorial programme on both floor levels.

noteworthy that the swallows are either feeding their young in the nests or courting. There can be no doubt then about the time of the year indicated: it must be the spring.

Other elements on the frescoes suggest the same season. The iris on the pin in the hair of the wounded girl is a spring flower. The lilies embroidered on the blouse of one of the older women (fig. 45) and the wild roses carried by the same figure are spring flowers. In view of the above, I believe that the crocus of the frescoes is part of a spring landscape. Lilac crocuses do grow in the spring although admittedly they are much rarer than the autumn variety. I believe that here naturalism has been sacrificed to symbolism. The presence of these various flowers suggests a rebirth of nature after the barren winter period.

Some additional elements support this hypothesis. The W. wall of the upper storey of room 3 was painted with a marshy landscape with reeds and flying ducks (fig. 44). Part of this fresco, of which only small fragments are published in *Thera* VII, depicted also a fowling scene where birds are caught in nets.

The significance of these scenes can be understood with reference to a specific detail, namely the necklace of the goddess presiding over the crocus gatherers (fig. 49). It will be remembered that the latter fresco was in the same room on the same floor. The necklace consisted of three rows of beads, ducks and insects. I have

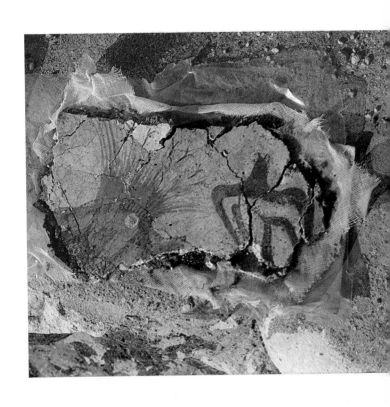

45. Older woman carrying flowers,
room 3, Xeste 3. Upper
floor S. (?) wall.

46. Older woman with a crocus costume,
room 3, Xeste 3. Upper
floor S. (?) wall.

47. Fresco fragment depicting a swallow
and a nest; frieze from Xeste 3.

48. Ritual vase from Xeste 3 depicting
flying swallows, lilies and crocuses.

49. Sketch of the goddess from the Crocus Gatherers fresco. She is wearing a necklace with ducks and dragonflies; room 3, Xeste 3. Upper floor N. wall.

identified the latter as dragonflies. Both of these are connected with marshes and lakes so that the goddess of the crocus landscape, who is also wearing a crocus costume, is at the same time the goddess of life in the marshes. It is correct, therefore, to call her a mistress of nature. She is, in fact, a thematic link between the marshy scene and the Crocus Gatherers fresco.

What is the meaning of the marshy landscape? Birds caught in nets provide food for humans. Fowling scenes in marshes are common in Egyptian tombs and their significance there is similar (fig. 50). In the Egyptian landscapes fowl and fish of different kinds abound and are made available to the dead as life-sustaining elements. In the words of Groenewegen-Frankfort: "...abundance meant throughout not only possessions and a surfeit of food, but a joyful awareness of earth's fecundity, of beasts and plants..." (*Arrest and Movement,* p. 82).

Is it an accident than in the Egyptian marshy scenes dragonflies abound (fig. 50)? I think not: in Egypt as well as in Thera plants, animals and insects of these landscapes are symbols of the fertility of nature.

50. Egyptian fowling scene in the marshes; tomb of Nakht, Thebes.
Note especially the ducks and dragonflies.

I shall now attempt an overall interpretation of the nature frescoes trying to connect the flower scenes with the marshy landscape. I suggest that the idea behind the iconographical programme was the various aspects and manifestations of the renewal of nature in the spring. Swallows court and feed their young. Birds and insects abound, flowers spring forth from the earth. The fertility of nature is celebrated in various ways. The necklace of the goddess with ducks and dragonflies and her crocus costume crystallize this image in art.

It remains to relate the initiation of the young girls to this general context of nature's renewal, because it is clear that the initiation festival in question takes place in the spring. It is as though nature provided a model for womanhood, because in the mythopoeic mind fertility of the earth and child-bearing are analogous and related phenomena. The time when plants and beasts grow is an appropriate one for the young girls to enter their new role.

The above is suggested by the frescoes from rooms 2, 4 and 3 of Xeste 3. I have tried to show that they form a coherent pictorial programme of independent but related themes which revolve around nature and womanhood.

I shall finish by citing an analogous festival well-attested in our sources. It is the festival of the *Thesmophoria* which was celebrated in Classical Athens in the autumn in honour of the corn goddess Demeter. It was connected with the planting and sowing season and was strictly confined to women.

This three-day celebration culminated in a ritual called *Kalligeneia* which refers to "fair offspring". Demeter, though chiefly the goddess of corn, presided also over human fertility as H. W. Parke has observed. It is, therefore, not surprising that fertility of women was connected with an agricultural festival. I also believe that *Kalligeneia* involved young women, although this is not accepted by everyone. However, it seems improbable to me that "fair offspring" would be celebrated in connection with mature women who would have given birth already or would even have been past reproductive age. It makes more sense if the ritual in question was mostly for the sake of young, prospective mothers. If that is the case, then the *Kalligeneia* may well have included an aspect of initiation. Thus, the *Thesmophoria* provides a good parallel for the reconstructed festival depicted on the frescoes from Xeste 3. Both are vegetation festivals, in both women are the protagonists, in both there is a strong emphasis on fertility.

The sum up: we have looked at two Theran festivals as they are represented on the frescoes. In one the protagonists are men; in the other women. In both social hierarchy and role division are apparent. Finally, it is evident in both cases that Minoan society moved in harmony with the seasonal cycles.

51. Plan of Xeste 3.

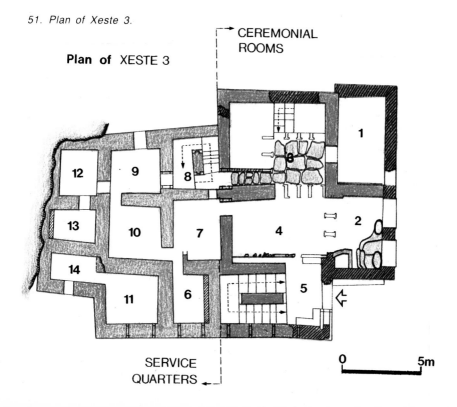

Plan of XESTE 3

CEREMONIAL ROOMS

12 9 8 3 1

13 10 7 4 2

14 11 6 5

SERVICE QUARTERS

0   5m

CHAPTER VI

Initiation, Vegetation and Sacrifice: The Adyton Fresco of Xeste 3

In the previous chapter, the pictorial progamme of Xeste 3 has been related to a festival which celebrated the renewal of nature and in which initiation of young girls was involved. Here, the adyton fresco will be examined more closely and a reconstruction of the rituals will be attempted on the basis of pictorial and architectural elements.

Architecturally the *adyton* (holy of holies) is the focal point of the ground floor (fig. 5). It is placed at the N. end of the building and separated from the entrance by a series of rooms interconnected by means of multiple doors *(polythyra)*. A detailed architectural analysis of the rooms would be out of place here, therefore, only a few elements which are relevant to the cult activities will be touched upon.

1. Rooms 2, 3, 4 and 7 are fairly large and could accommodate many people (see also ch. II) (fig. 51).

2. The *adyton* could be screened from common view if the doors of the surrounding rooms were closed. The screening could be effected in varying degrees. For example, the best view would be afforded to those standing in room 3, a less good view to those standing in 4, while the participants in 2 and 7 would be off the axis of vision and would thus be standing on the periphery of the action. On the other hand, nothing of the action in the *adyton* would be visible even to those in room 3 if the doors of the former were shut. In short, the architectural design of the building was intended to allow successive admittance into the vicinity of the *adyton*.

3. The ground and upper floor of Xeste 3 have identical plans. Since the construction of superimposed *polythyra* (practically hollow walls) involves solving difficult engineering problems, there must have been a serious reason behind this choice of construction. If architecture reflects function, we can postulate a similar, indeed a parallel, action taking place on both floors.

4. There were two stairways in the building situated in different sections. One, the larger, was placed near the entrance (5 on the plan) and must have been intended for public use. The other, the smaller, was in the vicinity of the adyton (8 on the plan) and was probably intended for more intimate use by the personnel or the initiates. If there was a sequence of parallel actions on both floors, the stairways would have allowed the public, on the one hand, and the select few, on the other, to proceed separately to the upper storey.

5. The *adyton* was a place of separation. The latter would be effected through descent which placed the descending person on a different level to the rest of the participants. This action may have had a symbolic significance, namely, contact with the earth or the underworld. Nothing in the architecture or in the fresco suggest purification or use of water. The usual term "Lustral Basin", invented by Evans for similar structures in Crete, does not apply at all to the Akrotiri *adyton* (see also ch. II).

52. *Sketch of the adyton fresco depicting three girls on the N. wall
and an altar on the E. wall; room 3, Xeste 3.*

This brief architectural survey shows that the building was suitable for cult
activities of a mystical character. The focal point was the *adyton* and its fresco.

This fresco is the most difficult to understand. This is because the content is
neither purely narrative nor purely ritual but a mixture of both. The N. wall depicts
three girls (figs. 43, 52), the E. wall an altar topped with horns of consecration (fig.
53). Although the girls would be visible to most people standing in or around 3, it
was the altar which was the focal point for those descending into the *adyton*. The
reason is that the hypothetical person would have to turn eastwards by necessity,
following the direction of the stairs, and would thus be facing the altar.

The altar fresco was, therefore, just as important as the one with the girls in terms
of ritual significance. It is important to note two points about the altar. The first is its
decoration of lilies which connects it with spring and vegetation, and which fits with
the general hypothesis proposed in the previous chapter that the iconographical
programme of the building is full of spring symbolism. The second, and most
important point, is that a red substance is trickling from the horns down the altar;
this is most probably blood. The inevitable conclusion is that a blood libation is
depicted. It is almost certain that such were practised in Crete as the iconographical evidence suggests. On the sarcophagus of Hagia Triada (fig. 15), for example, a
bucket is placed below the sacrificial animal to receive its blood. Collection of blood
can hardly have any purpose other than blood libations.

To return to the altar fresco of the E. wall. Given the above, we can assume that
sacrifice is alluded to by the blood trickling from the horns of consecration, and that

the altar is shown here in connection with a ritual practice. Another observation suggests this hypothesis. The sacred structure seems to be the terminal walking point for many of the figures depicted on the walls of room 3 and the *adyton* itself. Starting from the latter, the left girl (westernmost one) is holding a necklace and is walking eastward (fig. 52). There can be no other destination for the offering of the necklace than the altar of the E. wall. Thus, the figure can be seen as an abbreviated procession reminiscent of the walking adorants carrying fish from

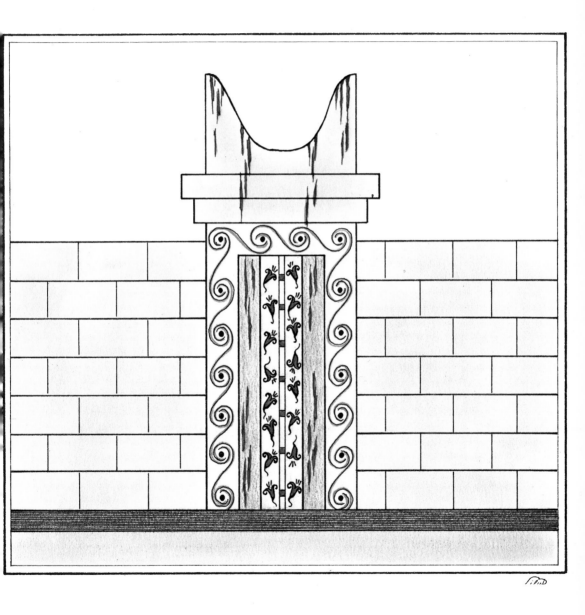

53. Altar on the E. wall, room 3, ground floor, Xeste 3.

54. *Tentative reconstruction of the W. section of room 3 which had polythyra*
and was possibly a treasury. The position of the frescoes is uncertain.
The middle doors are shown closed in the reconstruction.

the West House (ch. IV) or the woman from the Costuming Scene from the House of
the Ladies to be discussed further on (ch. VIII). In addition, there were males
decorating the W. wall of room 3 (fig. 54). In the previous chapter I have designated
them as marginal participants in the festival. Although they have not been finally
restored yet, it is clear that they are carrying objects (vases, a piece of cloth) and
that they are walking in a N. direction. Had they been able to walk around the wall,
they would have reached the *adyton* and the altar fresco. Finally, the right

(eastermost) girl of the N. wall of the fresco has a shaved head and is wrapped in a veil (figs. 52, 55). She has her back turned towards the two other girls and is looking towards the altar directing the spectator's attention there. In summary, many of the figures of the frescoes are either walking or looking towards the altar. Now, given the fact that the architectural area which this fresco covers is the *adyton*, it is reasonable to postulate a ritual equivalence. Could it be that objects, like those carried by the figures to the altar, were deposited in the *adyton* as offerings? This is

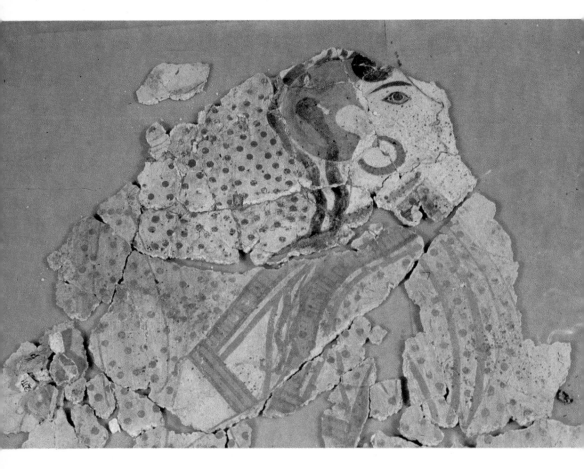

55. Girl lifting her veil and looking towards the altar in surprise.
From the adyton, room 3, Xeste 3.

a reasonable hypothesis because the W. section of room 3 is transversed by clay partitions and is modelled like a repository (fig. 54). It is, in fact, very reminiscent of the repositories next to the *adyton* (conventionally called Lustral Basin) of the palace at Zakros, Crete. The Xeste 3 repositories were found empty but this is not surprising. Had they contained valuable objects, these would have been the first to have been carried away after the earthquake.

The ritual reconstructed so far, on the basis of the frescoes and the repositories, is that offerings may have been carried, displayed and deposited by males and females. Since only females are depicted on the *adyton* fresco, they were clearly the protagonists. The ritual is more complicated than that, however. As mentioned above, the N. wall fresco is a mixture of narrative and ritual and we shall now turn our attention to this painting in an attempt to decipher it.

Of the three girls of the N. wall fresco, the central one is clearly the most important (figs. 56 and 52). This is indicated both by her central position and by the fact that she is approximately on the same vertical axis as the goddess of the fresco

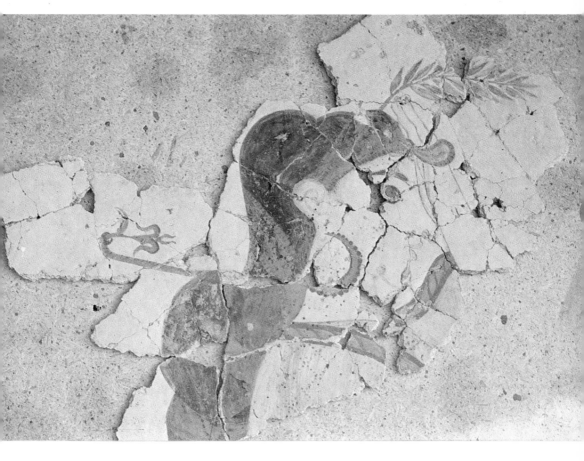

56. Head of the wounded girl from the adyton fresco, room 3, Xeste 3.

on the upper floor (fig. 40). Moreover, she stands out because of her unusual, dramatic posture. She is holding her right foot with her right hand while with the left hand she is thouching her forehead in a gesture of pain. Blood drips from her wounded foot; it is, thus, clear that the girl has had an accident. A crocus flower, fallen next to her, shows that she was engaged in flower gathering prior to the accident. In addition, she is ornamented with flowers and plants: she has an iris pin in her hair and a myrtle or olive branch is fastened above her forehead.

What is the significance of the wound? Before an answer is attempted, the following points must be mentioned. Firstly, the incident cannot represent a casual accident in the fields. This would be incompatible with the nature of Minoan art in which there is no room for the trivial or the incidental. What corroborates this view is that the scene lacks dramatic coherence and unity of action. The tragedy of the girl is self-contained in her own attitude and dramatic gesture. Her companions do not seem to be aware of her pain since one is looking towards the altar, whereas the other is carrying a necklace to it. Thus, if the wounding alludes to a story or myth, this is subordinated to a general ritual action and acquires its significance in relation to it. As we shall see, this ritual action is connected with initiation through encounter with blood/death.

Secondly, the wounded girl is associated with vegetation as her plant ornaments and the crocus flower beside her show. If there is an allusion to a Minoan myth, a vegetation figure was likely to have been involved.

Finally, there is a thematic echo of blood between the N. and E. wall frescoes of the adyton (fig. 51). The blood dripping from the girl's foot is paralleled by the blood trickling down the horns of consecration An equivalence between animal sacrifice/blood-libation and the human wounding is suggested.

The reading of the fresco engenders multiple associations between young girls, vegetation, blood and sacrifice. Can one arrive at a coherent interpretation of the cultic reality behind this complex nexus of ideas?

The first attempt at disentangling the mystery will involve a mythological investigation. If behind the wounded figure is a story, could it possibly have survived into Greek times? Indeed there are two myths with the same theme that may fit the pattern. These are the myths of Persephone and Eurydice which, despite their different details, have common themes. Both heroines were in the fields before they encountered fatal accidents. Persephone was abducted by Hades, the god of the underworld, while she was picking flowers. Eurydice while fleeing from her pursuer, was bitten by a snake in her foot and died as a result. Both had attendants, other young girls — a detail which is reminiscent of initiation rituals. It can be supposed that these two stories are variations on the same theme and that they may contain elements of ritual patterns such as "initiation through encounter with death". The latter is a well attested pattern of *rites de passage* as A. van Gennep has shown. The novice has to die symbolically in order to be born again in a new life and assume a new identity. Assuming then that initiation rituals of this kind are connected with the Persephone and Eurydice myths, what relationship do the latter have to the Bronze Age painting from Thera? I am not suggesting that the fresco represents either of these myths in its exact details. It is clear that there are differences as it is also clear that the myth could not have survived from the Bronze Age into the Classical period intact. Myths are products of social, historical and religious components which evolve in time. It must, therefore, be noted that the crystallization of the Persephone and Eurydice myths took place in an historical and social context much different from the Bronze Age one, and it is understandable that the details do not fit. It is justifiable methodologically, however, to postulate that the original idea was a Minoan one and that it made sense in a Minoan context. To support the last statement, I would like to draw attention to the vegetation element which is present both on the fresco and in the myths since the heroines of the latter are in the fields and Persephone is picking flowers before she is abducted by Hades. The relationship of vegetation to initiation has already been touched upon in the last chapter. Death and rebirth of nature is a phenomenon analogous to initiation which involves the taking up of a new life and role. The time of womanhood has to coincide with the reawakening of nature in the spring symbolized by flowers and plants. A. van Gennep, who has written one of the classic works on rites of passage, has collected many examples from "primitive cultures" where this same association is illustrated:

> "Rites of passage which conform to the usual pattern are found in the ceremonies pertaining to the seasons which often fall at the time of the summer or winter solstices...
>
> Often the expulsion of winter is a rite of separation, bringing in summer into the village a rite of incorporation... It follows that an exact parallel to purely seasonal rites of passage may be found in rites intended to assure the rebirth of vegetation after the transitional period of winter dormancy..." (*Rites of Passage,* p. 179).

We see, then, that vegetation festivals, far from being incompatible with initiation rites, can provide the framework in which the latter take place.

Let us now attempt a synthesis of the above observations and try to reconstruct the initiation ritual.

The *adyton* fresco provides us with significant clues. Upon careful observation, one notes that the three girls depicted there are differentiated by hairstyle and costume which is indicative of age and hierarchy. The right girl with the veil, for example, must be the youngest and not yet initiated. Her hair is still partially shaved and her flounced kilt is short: part of her legs are bare. Moreover, no breasts are visible. The left girl, carrying the necklace, on the other hand, has full breasts, long hair and her skirt, worn under the kilt, reaches her feet. She is older and probably already initiated. The central girl with the wounded foot is the one who wears the most unusual costume. She has full length hair and full breasts. Due to her position in the centre of the fresco and because of the mythical associations evoked by the wounded foot, I believe she is the initiate. She is impersonating the vegetation goddess and undergoes the same suffering. In reality the initiate may have had to be scratched in the foot so that some token blood would flow.

Close relations between myths and rituals are amply documented. Suffice it to mention two instances here. In the Eleusinian mysteries the search for Persephone and her return were somehow reflected in the initiation rituals of the Telesterion at Eleusis. At the sanctuary of Artemis at Brauron, young girls of about the age of initiation had to serve the goddess for a term. Before they were released, they were scratched on the neck so that blood would flow, a practice which was explained by the following myth. Artemis demanded human sacrifice in exchange for one of her bears which had been killed by men. Here, also, we have initiation, symbolic death, actualized by blood flow, and a myth.

To return to the Theran practices. The girls were probably gathered in the area before the *adyton.* Of the fresco only the oldest girl with the necklace (on the left) would be visible if all the doors of the *adyton* were closed (fig. 57). But when its doors opened, the wounded girl and the pre-initiate would be successively revealed because there is a spacial correspondence between the doors and the figures painted on the wall. Thus, we can postulate a sequence of successive visual revelations with emphasis on seeing. Veiling may also have been involved as we can infer from the veiled pre-initiate; besides we know that veiling was practiced during many mysteries, including the Eleusinian ones.

57. *Tentative reconstruction of the adyton. The screen construction in front of the fresco controlled the visual accessibility.*

The culmination of the ceremony must have involved sight of the altar with the trickling blood when one entered the adyton. As noted above, a symbolic scratching of the foot may have been an accompanying ritual. These experiences must have taken place in an atmosphere of awe, mystery and even terror. There was only dim light in the area as there are not many windows; lamps found there testify to the same conclusion. The psychological experience must have been deep. After it, the initiate was released into a new life and a new identity.

Offerings, carried from the adjacent treasury, would have formed part of the ritual but we cannot know at what stage this took place (fig. 57).

The polarity between renewal of life and death is expressed visually on the fresco by the juxtaposition of blood and flowers. This is visible both on the altar and on the wounded girl who is adorned with plants. Blood evokes ideas of sacrifice and death, flowers of life and regeneration. The cultic reality also juxtaposes these two elements by combining sacrificial rituals with festivals of vegetation, renewal and initiation.

In conclusion, the frescoes of the *adyton* and the neighbouring walls give us some clues about the ritual performed in the building. The *adyton* must be seen as a place of separation; descent into it might have even carried connotations of contact with the earth or the underworld. We have seen that objects were carried and possibly placed in it by both sexes, although females were clearly the protagonists. In reconstructing the ceremonies, we must also take into account the identical floor plans of both the ground floor and upper storey. It is possible that one stage of the ritual involved contact with blood, wounding, sacrifice and carrying of objects. But when people climbed to the upper storey, by means of the stairways of the building, they saw quite a different sight and a very different fresco decoration. The focal point was not a wounded girl or an altar, but the goddess seated on her tripartite platform and supervising crocus gathering. She was surrounded by lush landscapes, ducks, a fowling scene and women carrying floral offerings (fig. 40). The prevailing idea was one of fecundity and renewal represented by landscape scenes and floral offerings made by women. Whereas the frescoes of the ground floor represent ritual, those of the upper storey transport us into typical Minoan landscapes of a dream world.

CHAPTER VII

Landscape Scenes

Few have missed the importance of landscapes in Minoan art. The quality of movement and colours, the variety of shapes of the animals and plants create an impression of a dreamland. In this art nature is convincing, not frozen and rigid.

Such scenes are very often present on Minoan frescoes whatever the subject might be. In fact there are only a few representations where the action takes place in an architectural setting rather than in nature. Still accuracy of depiction and realism was not the strength of the Aegean artists. The few plants which can be identified with certainty, such as lilies and crocuses, exhibit unnatural traits, hybridism or stylization, and much of the flora is not identifiable at all. O. Rackham has observed that most lilies are a combination of the white Madona Lily *(Lilium candidum)* and the red lily *(Lilium chalcedonicum)*. The ivy which appears on frescoes from Crete as well as on the frescoes of the Antelopes and Boxing Children from Thera (fig. 73) is no plant known to science. It seems that nature was either drawn from memory or from pattern books. At any rate, the artists were not interested in accuracy but only in the general impression. The latter, however, is definitely convincing.

The most noteworthy achievement of Minoan nature scenes is the organic way in which nature fuses with human action creating a proper setting for it. A comparison with Mesopotamian and Mycenaean art might prove illuminating. The Assyrians for example, make frequent use of landscape but they use it to merely indicate location. Trees and plants appear lifeless and disproportionately small compared to the humans. The result is static pictures where humans are the main subject and where nature has only a subordinate role. The same observation can be made also about Mycenaean art. On a fresco fragment from Tiryns, where a chariot with two women is depicted, trees are rendered like peg poles devoid of any naturalism; they are only meant as landscape signs. Minoan nature scenes are strikingly different in this respect. The colours alone involuntarily draw the spectator's attention to the animals and plants as for example on the Partridge Frieze from Knossos (fig. 58). Why is nature so important in Minoan art? We shall see that it is not unrelated to religious attitudes and perceptions of the world. First, however, it should be stressed that landscapes cannot be merely decorative, a kind of wallpaper, as is sometimes argued. This is incompatible with the mentality of the period since art was serious and functional. Also it does not accord with the archaeological evidence because in Thera cult equipment was found in the rooms decorated with such scenes.

The contexts of landscapes are crucial for a correct assessment of their significance. Yet, from Crete we have only fragments. This has had serious implications for the understanding of Minoan art because these fragments have often been perceived as independent panels and only very seldom has it been realized that there were other figures, human or divine, in the same composition. A

58. *Partridge frieze from the Karavanserai at Knossos.*

good example is the famous cat fresco from Hagia Triada. This is often admired and reproduced but very rarely is it pointed out that it was part of a larger composition decorating a room of the villa. I shall quote from Sinclair Hood's book on *The Arts in Prehistoric Greece* because he gives as complete a description as can be expected considering the fragmentary state of the fresco. His ideas are a result of collaboration with M. Cameron.

> Three sides of the room seem to have been decorated with a scene reaching from floor to ceiling. On the narrow end wall a woman, evidently a goddess, wearing a richly decorated skirt, may have stood before a shrine. Rocky, flower-bedecked landscapes occupied the side walls. On the wall to the left as one faced the goddess at the end of the room was a woman, an attendant it seems, kneeling and perhaps engaged in picking sacred flowers such as lilies and crocuses. The landscape on the opposite wall was filled with animals, among them cats and apparently wild goats. A large fragment which is exceptionally well preserved although discoloured by fire, shows a cat stalking a small but elegant red bird with a long black tail (pp. 52-53).

The important points to note in the preceding description are the identification of the room as a shrine, the existence of the goddess in the natural setting and the presence of human participants in relation to a ceremony. Women pick flowers in order to offer them to the goddess. Although much of this is restoration, it is confirmed by the existence of a parallel fresco from Thera, the Crocus Gatherers (fig. 40).

Another good example of a misunderstood fragment is the one depicting flying-fish from Phylakopi, Melos. Although the liveliness of the fish is often commented upon, it

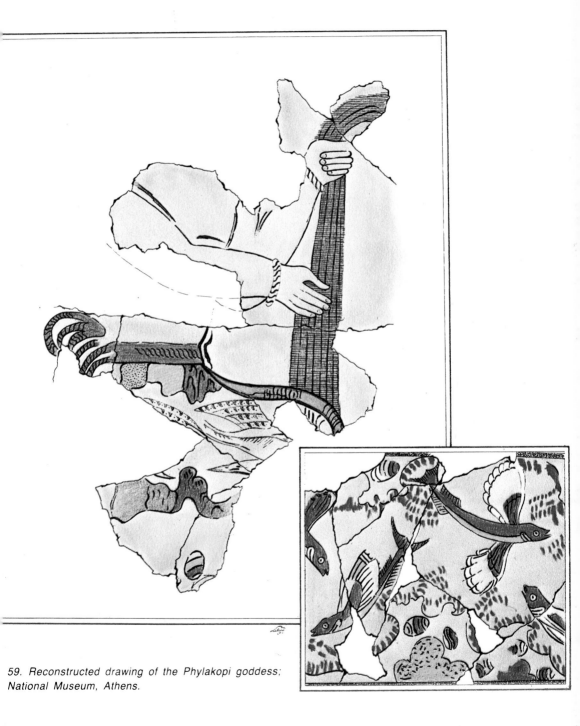

59. *Reconstructed drawing of the Phylakopi goddess;*
National Museum, Athens.

60. *Offering table painted with crocuses, from Akrotiri.*

61. *Reconstruction of the painting from the House of the Frescoes,*
Knossos, by M.A.S. Cameron.

is only seldom that one reads that there was a large female figure, holding a fishing net(?) depicted on a fragment found with the fish. She was probably a goddess and I suspect that her dress was adorned with a landscape (fig. 59). If so, the goddess is the protectress of nature as a whole.

A confirmation of this supposition, relating the goddess to landscapes which indicate her natural environment, comes from Thera. In the Crocus Gatherers Fresco (fig. 40), which has been described in the previous chapters, the goddess is depicted in a rocky terrain in which crocuses grow. Girls pick the flowers and offer them to the goddess. The Hagia Triada mural with the Cat fresco has the same elements: nature, a goddess and flower gathering women.

A pattern seems to develop. The female deity is shown in nature surrounded by the living beings of her domain whether they be monkeys, griffins, birds, cats, fish, or humans. It is instructive that the Minoans and Therans imagine the deity in her natural environment rather than in a temple as was often the case with Mesopotamian depictions.

I would now like to explore the possibility of symbolism which may be involved in the depiction of certain flowers and plants. It is a fact that, given the immense variety of wild flowers which grow in Greece, only a few are consistently depicted on Minoan frescoes and pottery. The most common of these are lilies and crocuses which are especially popular in Thera. Others are iris, papyrus, wild rose *(cistus)*, myrtle, olive, palm, rushes, ivy, poppy, etc. Some of these flowers may be considered sacred in the sense that they are offered to the goddess. Crocuses, for example, decorate offering tables from Thera (fig. 60), lilies decorate an altar on a fresco from Xeste 3 (fig. 52). Lilies appear on an altar on a seal from Routsi, Peloponnese. These few instances prove the sacred use of the flowers. But why these particular plants? One

62. Lilies fresco from room Δ 2.

reason is aesthetic. The beauty of crocuses and lilies is striking. They are also fragrant and this was an important factor in religious experience. I would like to suggest an additional factor: territorial distribution. Crocuses and lilies grow in rocky terrain, on mountains and hills. Papyri and rushes are indicative of rivers and marshes. This classification is clear on Theran frescoes. In room 5 of the West House there was a frieze depicting a river landscape (fig. 25). The recognizable plants are palms and papyri. On the other hand the rocky landscapes from Δ2 (fig. 62) and Xeste 3 depict lilies and crocuses respectively. Within room 3 of Xeste 3 (upper storey) the division is apparent within the same room: crocuses and rushes decorate different walls (fig. 4).

There is one fresco from Knossos, however, which depicts all these plants and many others together. I see it as a symbolic landscape suggestive of the renewal of nature. This is the painting from the House of the Frescoes at Knossos (fig. 61). It consists of many fragmentary pieces which M. Cameron has restored as a continuous frieze, depicting monkeys, birds and many types of plants, among which crocuses, lilies, iris, ivy, papyri and rushes may be distinguished. At first glance there may seem nothing different about this fresco, but upon close inspection certain inconsistencies appear which show that the depiction is conceptual rather than realistic. First of all there are so many plants and flowers, that an "orgy of vegetation" is suggested. Second, the flowers of different terrains and the terrains themselves are depicted side by side, which could never be the case in reality. Rivers and waterfalls are present and next to them papyri and reeds; rocks with lilies and crocuses appear in the immediate vicinity. Thus a compression of nature is accomplished within one single painting. M. Cameron has suggested that the birds may be courting. If this is so, there is an added allusion to spring and hence regeneration of nature.

It might seem an exaggeration to designate the above paintings as a symbolic depiction of the ideal spring. Yet, "religious landscapes", as H. Frankfort has called them, exist in Egyptian art. They are analyzed by Frankfort as follows in his book on *Ancient Egyptian Religion* (p. 154):

> The Egyptian religious landscape was a vast expanse of marsh. It is almost ubiquitous in religious literature. It is present in the belief in an afterlife as the Field of Rushes. It is the scene in which the ancient image of the mother-goddess Hathor, the wild cow, manifests herself by parting the reeds with her head.
>
> Lotus and papyrus were essential constituents of this unchanging significant "landscape of the first time". It was not their perishable nature that impressed the Egyptians; on the contrary, the decay of the individual plants was a meaningless incident in comparison with the perennial presence of the species in the scenery from which the universe had gone forth, and which was a reality everpresent in man's thought through the religious imagery which we have mentioned.

It seems to me that the frieze from the House of the Frescoes was such a landscape. In the room where it stood a stone offering table and a votive ladle inscribed in Linear A were found; therefore, it must have been a shrine.

63. Lilies fresco from Δ2, detail.

The Fresco of the Lilies from Thera (fig. 62). The fresco was a large composition decorating three walls of room Δ2 which was situated on the ground floor. The scene depicts spectacular rocks from which lilies grow. The red flowers are in triple sets and are depicted in various stages of growth. Some are buds whereas others are fully open. The picture is not static: it is enlivened by flying swallows and by the bending stalks of the lilies which give the impression that a light breeze blows through them. The scene is, therefore, naturalistic but it is inaccurate and not realistic. The rocks have exaggerated shapes and colours. I am not at all convinced by the suggestion that they depict a typical pre-eruption Thera setting. Rather they represent the idea of rocky ground using the conventions of

Minoan art. Moreover, the lilies are all erect, although this is an unnatural position for the buds which stoop on real plants. As noted above, the intention of the painters was to convince, not to reproduce reality. The aim behind this work of art is to suggest the coming of spring as Sp. Marinatos immediately perceived: "It wants to express the advanced spring season when the swallows... are restless from mating fever and are feverishly preparing their nests" (*Thera* IV, 50). The association of lilies or crocuses with swallows is frequent in Theran art (fig. 63) appearing on frescoes as well as on pottery (fig. 48) and it certainly alludes to the reawakening of nature in the spring.

Granted that there is symbolism involved in the painting, why not include the goddess herself? We have seen in the survey of Minoan frescoes above that nature scenes are often the environment of the goddess or they are a background for ritual action as is the case in the Olive Grove fresco from Knossos. Is the Lilies fresco an exception? My belief is that the purpose of the landscape is similar here also. The main difference is that cult activity is not part of the painting, rather it takes place in front of it . We must imagine the fresco as a backdrop for ritual action serving a function similar to that of a scenic backdrop in a theatre in front of which the plot develops.

This hypothesis is verified by the archaeological evidence. In the Lilies room Δ2 a sickle and bags containing flour were found. In front of the room there was a millstone. It must be mentioned that the bags with flour were moved there by the squatters after the earthquake so that their presence could theoretically be unconnected with the original function of the room. Yet, the existence of the millstone and the sickle proves that there was a connection between the Lilies' room and agricultural activities. It is reasonable, therefore, to identify Δ2 as a shrine where rituals connected with a harvest festival and/or the grinding of grain took place. The nature scene in the background fulfilled an important purpose: it perpetuated and ensured the regeneration of nature.

The other fresco from Akrotiri depicting only plants is the Papyrus fresco from the Room of the Ladies, in the House of the Ladies (fig. 64). It decorated the W. wall and parts of the N. and S. walls of a room and existed alongside another fresco depicting women. The latter will be discussed further on; suffice it to say that the women were involved in ritual action and that the theme of the frescoes suggests that the room was a shrine. Indeed, ritual vessels existed in four repositories which were sealed under the floor of the Papyrus room. More cult equipment was found in the adjacent store-room 7. Thus both frescoes and finds leave little doubt that the room was used for cult purposes. The Papyri then apparently depict another "religious landscape".

Papyrus was in all probability not indigenous to Thera although it is possible that it grew in Crete. Even there, however, it could not have been a common plant. It is explicable, therefore, that this flower is even more stylized than others and it is quite clear that the iconographical form was derived from Egypt. In Egyptian paintings the plant is shown without leaves, as it should be (fig. 50). In the Theran

64. Papyrus fresco from the House of the Ladies.

one, however, leaves are added to the stem, which can be taken as one more proof that the artists had not seen real papyri but borrowed the iconographical type from Egypt, probably via Crete.

The question is what the symbolic significance of the plant is in Minoan and Theran art. Its popularity in Egypt is explained by its aquatic nature since river waters were the major sources of fertility there. In the Aegean, papyri are consistently associated with rivers or marshes and this might indicate that in this case also they have associations of fertility. On Thera, the two examples of frescoes where the plant is depicted are the E. Frieze, room 5, West House (fig. 25), and the room (or shrine) of the Ladies (fig. 64). In both cases a river is indicated. Although the latter is not clearly discernible in the Papyrus fresco from the Ladies' House (fig. 64), it can be argued that the undulating lines rendered in bands of different colours at the bottom of the fresco indicate a river. On an inlaid dagger from Mycenae, papyri grow again next to a river. Even as a pottery motif the plant in question grows in connection with undulating lines, below which hooklets are visible. As W. Niemeier has shown, these hooklets are a convention indicating swampy ground or rivers; they are most evident on the E. Frieze from Akrotiri (fig. 25).

One more point supports the idea that papyri had a symbolic significance in Minoan art: their association with a fantastic animal, the griffin. Papyri and griffins occur together on the E. Frieze, room 5, West House (fig. 25), as well as on the wall painting from the Throne Room in the palace of Knossos.

In conclusion, nature scenes in Minoan art are more symbolic than naturalistic. They allude to the general concept of fertility and fecundity in the spring. Very often they provide a setting for the appearance of the Minoan goddess and for ritual action; at other times they are just the background for cult activities which take place in the room in which they were painted.

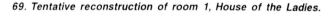

69. Tentative reconstruction of room 1, House of the Ladies.

CHAPTER VIII

Dressing the Priestess: The Frescoes of the Ladies

The Ladies' frescoes were found in a room which was named after them by Sp. Marinatos "Room of the Ladies". It was the N. section of a large free-standing building towards the N. of the settlement (fig. 65).

A little will be said about the surroundings of this area in order to elucidate its function. It was flanked by two rooms to the E. and.W. The W. one (no. 7 on the plan) was a magazine and it contained many cult vessels among which were rhyta, triton shells and nippled ewers (fig. 66). The E. room (no. 2 on the plan) must have been used for eating, since cooking pots and conical cups were found in it.

The room with the frescoes (no. 1 on the plan) communicated directly with the other two. It was connected with 2 by a door, although the existence of the latter has not yet been confirmed by excavations. A window set on the W. wall of room 1 was the means of communication with room 7. The window, in fact, interrupted the Papyrus murals (fig. 69). The main function of this window was not to let in light since it opened to another closed area. Rather, it was meant as a transaction window through which the cult vessels, stored in 7, would be handed into 1.

The central room 1 with the frescoes must have been a shrine, since a triton shell and conical cups were found in its vestibule. More important, however, is the existence of repositories below its floor in the W. part.

Why were the repositories under the floor and how could they be reached? It is possible that they were sealed off permanently after some important ritual, as was the case with the Temple Repositories at Knossos, and with the ritual pit at Vathypetro, Crete. The other possibility is that they were opened during important occasions through removal of the flagstones, a process both complicated and laborious. At any rate, the existence of these repositories shows that the painted room 1 had a religious function. The repositories were four in number and contained the following types of objects. Repository 1: cups; Rep. 2: four painted jugs, a rhyton, conical cups, a cooking pot; Rep. 3: a pot containing seeds, a jug decorated with a swallow. Regarding repository 4 it is stated that it contained nothing of importance. The assemblage of this pottery is significant suggesting offerings (rhyton), ritual eating (cooking pot, conical cups) and drinking (cups). What confirms this hypothesis is the existence of conical cups (which were used as plates) in the vestibule of the room, namely, the area with the Ladies' fresco. Here, too, the finds imply ritual activities, most probably drinking and offerings.

Thus, four factors point to the cultic function of the "Ladies' Room": frescoes, repositories, adjacent dining room, adjacent store-room with cult vessels.

The frescoes consisted of two groups depicting different subjects thus dividing the room into two sections with different fresco decoration. The E. part of the room was only a vestibule decorated with the Ladies qn facing walls, that is, the N. and S. walls (fig. 69.) Ch. Doumas has suggested that the vestibule was further subdivided by a

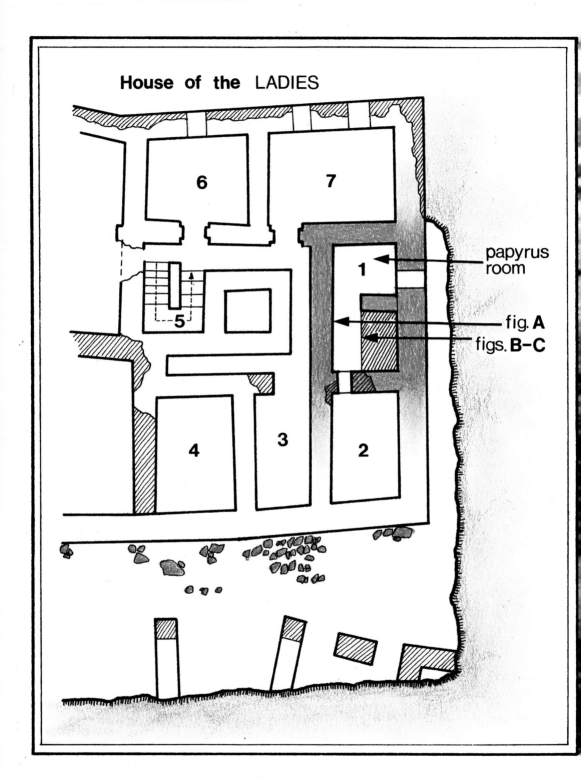

House of the LADIES

6

7

papyrus room

1

fig. A

figs. B–C

5

4

3

2

65. Plan of the House of the Ladies.

66. *Rhyta, from store-room 7, House of the Ladies.*

clay partition which would result in a fairly narrow corridor (see fig. 71). After passing through the corridor of the Ladies, the visitor would enter the part of the room decorated with Papyri (figs. 64, 69). This was undoubtedly the most important section of the shrine containing also the repositories.

A point about the orientation might be worth noting. The main shrine 5 of the West House also had its entrance from the East while the focal point of the cult was towards the West (fig. 31). Other similarities between the shrine of the West House and that of the Ladies exist. Room 5 had an accessory preparation room (4) just as this one has a vestibule. Both have dining areas. The West House shrine complex was larger however (see ch. IV).

The "Ladies" frescoes consist of two fragmentary groups depicting one female figure each. For reasons of convenience I shall refer to the N. wall figure as A and to the S. wall one as B (figs. 67 and 68).

67. Lady A, vestibule of room 1.
House of the Ladies.

Although they come from facing walls of the vestibule, it is certain that they belong to the same composition. Above both of them there is a similar decorative pattern composed of stars interspersed with red dots. It is noteworthy that the two women have similar hairstyles: long, dark hair. In addition they wear similar costumes and jewelry. Finally, they both wear rouge on their cheeks. This indicates similar status and shows that they are taking part in the same festive occasion.

A detailed examination of their dress is necessary as it bears directly on the problem of the restoration of a third figure. Both women wear a loose fitting robe with a deep *décolletage* which leaves the breasts exposed. This robe has decorative border bands edging the sleeves and the hem of the skirt. The band also bisects the front of the robe where presumably the seam was. It is important to note that what

68. Lady B, vestibule of room 1, House of the Ladies.

appears as a flounced skirt was actually a flounced kilt worn over the robe and tied with cords around the waist. Such cords are clearly visible on figures A and B. When the kilt was put on, the loose robe would cling to the body, giving the impression of a tight jacket (fig. 70).

We now turn to the question of what the women are doing. Figure A (fig. 67) is in a walking position moving towards the East. Could she walk, she would meet figure B (fig. 68) on the opposite wall. It is clear that she is holding something in her hands but this object is lost. It could be a piece of jewelry or some other ornament. Figure B has large, drooping breasts with a very prominent red nipple which may indicate that she is lactating. She is probably older than A but not old enough to have her hair tied in a bun. On her right hand she is holding a garment which can be identified

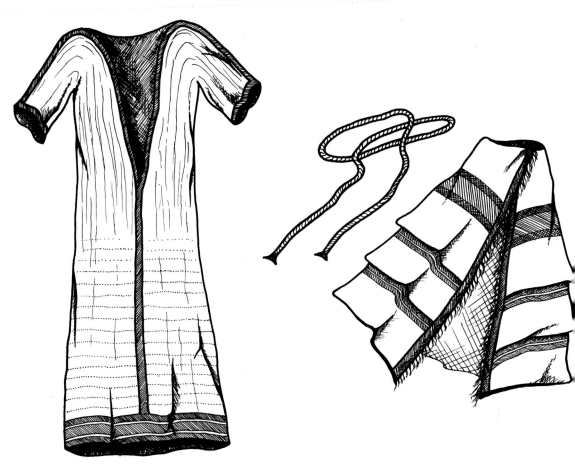

70. Reconstruction of the costume worn by the women on the frescoes.
(N.B. Fig. 69 = Fold-out B, between pp. 96-97).

as the flounced kilt described above (fig. 71). Of her left hand there is only a fragment, but enough has been left to show that she was touching something. Upon close inspection it can be seen that this is a sleeved arm. The characteristic decorative border band that we noted on the robes of ladies A and B is clearly visible here also (fig. 68). To the left of the sleeve there is something which looks like a veil made of thin material. I suggest that this is actually the bodice of the robe which is loose because it has not been girtled yet by the flounced kilt. This robe is worn by a third figure C. The kilt is being brought to her by Lady B and is about to be applied. It is certain that the third woman C was seated, since B is bending towards her. She was, however, larger than figure B which shows her higher status (figs. 68 and 71).

In conclusion, the Fresco of the Ladies can be described as a costuming scene, depicting a group of festively attired women bringing clothes and ornaments to a seated female. A sealing from Crete offers a parallel (*PM* IV, fig. 461). It remains to discuss who the seated woman is.

I would exclude the possibility that she is simply the lady of the house in her boudoir. Apart from arguments that have to do with the character of Aegean art we

71. Tentative reconstruction of room 1 showing the missing
figure C, probably a priestess.

must take into account the nature of the room in which the frescoes were found. There were repositories in room 1 and there was an adjacent magazine with cult equipment which does not suggest that this was a burgher's living-room or his wife's boudoir.

A second alternative, suggested by Sp. Marinatos, is that the woman C is a goddess. Yet, this also is unlikely in my opinion because of the position of the fresco in the vestibule. Had the goddess been depicted, a more appropriate place for the fresco would have been the main room, which, as we have seen, was decorated with papyri. There remains a third possibility: that figure C was a priestess who was about to be dressed and ornamented for some ceremony. This hypothesis fits the evidence best because it explains both the large size of figure C and the position of the fresco in the vestibule.

Reconstruction of the Ritual

The reconstruction of the ritual will be based on all the elements which have been discussed, namely, the arrangement of the rooms, the finds and the position of the frescoes. It is evident that only by a combination of all these factors can a real synthesis be achieved. The frescoes in particular offer invaluable clues but only if they are restored to their original position in the room. It would be natural to think, for example, that the most important composition was the Ladies. Artistically, in fact, it is clearly the most interesting one and it gives us most information about Aegean costumes and human forms. Yet, when restored in space we see that the Costuming Scene was secondary, since it was placed in the vestibule, it was the Papyri which had the most important function in relation to the cult.

The following can be deduced about the ritual. The Ladies' House had a shrine in which a ceremony was performed. This can be deduced by the elaborate attire of the women. The ritual involved preparations which included dressing up the priestess in the vestibule of the shrine as well as preparatory offerings which can be inferred from the presence of a triton shell and conical cups in the vestibule. Then the priestess would enter the Papyrus room where more offerings would take place. The cult implements for these would have been a *kymbe* painted with dolphins and horned animals, nippled ewers, rhyta, triton shells, etc., all of which were stored in the magazine (7) communicating with the shrine through the window. Another ritual can be inferred, during the course of which a cult meal would have been consumed, and of which evidence exists in the anteroom (2) of the shrine. As it will be remembered, a cooking pot and several conical cups were found there, while the same type of equipment was stored also in the sealed repositories of the Papyrus room. Now, the anteroom is situated in front of the shrine, not behind it. If the architectural arrangement of the rooms reflects the sequence of events; if, in other words, there is a correspondence between spatial and temporal sequences, then the cult meals should have taken place before the priestess entered the Papyrus room. Besides, there is a good reason for the anteroom (2) to be in front of the shrine. Presumably only the priestess (or at the most, a very few select people) would enter the main shrine, whereas more of the personnel would take part in the meal. This personnel would be part of the household of the "House of the Ladies" and would be in charge of the maintenance of the shrine. Only the qualified priestess, however, would be conducting the main offerings.

About the nature of the festival in question nothing can be said with certainty. I suspect that it had to do with the cycles of nature, however, because papyri are, after all, plants and it is the Papyri which dominate the shrine. In addition, seeds were found in a jar in the sealed repositories. Could that be symbolic of regeneration? This is conceivable, since the Egyptians regularly placed seeds which had been watered in tombs. When they germinated, resurrection was thought to take place. It is possible, therefore, that the repositories would be occasionally opened, in order to make the seeds germinate and simulate the regeneration of nature.

As for the significance of the papyrus, this has been discussed in a previous chapter (ch. VII). Here let it suffice to repeat that its Egyptian derivation is very probable and that the Minoans associated papyrus especially with waters.

CHAPTER IX

Animals and Humans: The Antelopes, Boxing Children and Monkey Frescoes

The Antelopes and Boxing Children

The first group of frescoes which will be discussed in this chapter composed the decorative scheme of B1. This was a room of modest size on the first storey of sector B (fig. 72). It must have been a shrine since it contained chest-like repositories which were made of low clay partitions. They were situated in the S. part of the room. In them were found two tables of offerings and other pottery.

Architecturally the shrine was subdivided into three sections by thin walls. Thus, there was B1: main shrine; B1a: repository; B1b: preparation room(?) (fig. 72). The main shrine contained a large window facing the square of the mill (see fig. 1). Through this window communication between the public gathered in the square and the shrine was possible. An adjacent room, B2, may have been used for dining since there was a kitchen store-room below it (fig. 6).

On the whole B1 resembles the other shrines which have been discussed above. It has a large window and a cupboard like the shrine of the West House; it has an adjacent dining area like the Papyrus and West House shrines. Finally, like the other two shrines, B1 has an entrance from the East.

The pictorial programme consisted of two themes: Antelopes and Boxing Children. It is certain that the Antelopes dominated the room, decorating most of the available space (figs. 73 and 78).

Although Sp. Marinatos identified the species of the animals as *Oryx Beissa,* it seems that in fact they are a hybrid of the Thompson and Grant Gazelle and also *Oryx Beissa.* It is thus probable that the iconographical form is derived from other pictures and that the painter had never seen the real animals. For this reason the artistic achievement is all the more impressive. The animals are rendered with surprising liveliness in simple, outline form.

There were six antelopes altogether, two pairs and two single (fig. 73). The animals in the pairs display animation which is evident by their raised tails and their half-open mouths. They are trotting side by side, the animal to the left is looking backwards towards the one to its right. Sp. Marinatos thought that the antelopes were courting and that they were engaged in amorous conversation. Although this is iconographically plausible, another explanation lies closer at hand. Firstly, it should be noted that the animals are of the same size, whereas the female of this species is somewhat smaller. But apart from this, the animosity displayed can be just as easily explained as competitive behaviour. It is well known that gazelles, as well as some antelopes, are territorial animals which compete for status. It can be objected, however, that had the intention of the artist been to depict conflict, the antelopes would have been shown facing each other since this is the usual position for fighting.

78. Tentative reconstruction of room B1 showing the W., N. and E. walls.

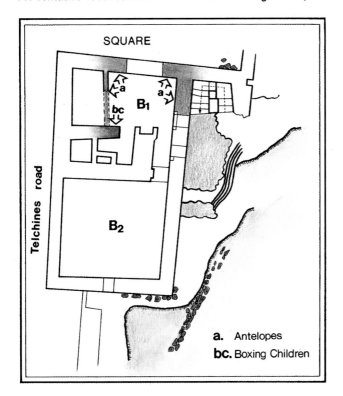

72. Plan of B1.

This, however, would have stressed the aggressive character of the scene beyond that which was desirable if mere competition not serious conflict was intended. Indeed, many horned animals avoid serious fighting which could result in fatal injuries. Instead they indulge in ritualized fighting which involves more innocuous contests. This is how the ethologist K. Lorenz describes the behavioural patterns of fallow deer:

73. Frescoes of the Antelopes and Boxing Children, room B1.

"In these animals, the highly ritualized antler fight... is preceeded by a broadside display in which both animals goose-step side by side at the same time nodding their heads to make the great antlers move up and down" (*On Aggression,* p.110).

It is clear from the above quote that competition is not always frontal among horned animals. But if the artist had never seen antelopes (or gazelles), it could be objected, how could he have known details of their behaviour? As we have seen

74. Sealing from Hagia Triada
showing two horned animals
racing, after V.E.G. Kenna.

already, however, Minoan artists drew upon traditional decorative schemes which may perhaps have been transmitted through pattern books or travelling artists. Nature was convincingly but not accurately rendered, as we have noted in the discussion about papyrus and other plants. Consequently, the artist's knowledge would have been derived from other pictures rather than real observation. Ready schemes, showing horned animals, would have been available from Crete. A sealing from Hagia Triada, for example, shows two horned animals running side by side in what Kenna describes as "play". There also one animal turns its head towards the other and the iconographical form is reminiscent of the Akrotiri Antelopes (fig. 74).

The Boxing Children were described by Sp. Marinatos as the main showpiece of B1 (fig. 75). Two children, about 7 or 8 years of age, are depicted with correct anatomical proportions, a rare achievement in ancient art. No sex differentiation is possible but it is likely that both are boys since they are painted red, the conventional colour indicating males. They are naked except for a belt with a dark loincloth hanging from it. Details of the loincloth are no longer visible due to the damaged condition of the fresco. A knot is discernible on top of the right boy's belt. Both have long, black hair-locks growing from blue skulls; as has been noted before this denotes partial shaving and youth (chs. IV and V). Boxing gloves are worn by both children on their right hands. The left boy has jewelry: earrings, bracelets, anklets and a necklace. No jewelry is visible on the extant fragments of the right boy. The left boy has a paler face than the right one. Given this and his jewelry, he must be of higher status than the other. Whether he is older or higher on the hierarchical scale must remain an open question.

All the elements suggest that the boxing was of a ritual nature and not just a children's game. The jewelry is one indication since the latter is worn on ceremonial occasions also on Cretan frescoes; the costume is another. It has been noted before that males with shaved heads are usually depicted naked at Akrotiri. This has been the case with both the adorants from the West House and with some of the males of room 3 in Xeste 3 (figs. 18 and 44). Yet, both the boxing boys are wearing a belt with a knot and a loincloth. Now this is a common male attire on Crete appearing on adorants as well as people engaged in sports: bull-leaping or boxing. Most notable is the similarity with the dress of men engaged in bull hunting on a circular ivory vase found at Katsamba, Crete (fig. 76). One man balances himself on the bull's horns whereas two other men are running away from the bull. All the men wear belts and loincloths; in addition knots, similar to that of the boxing child, are discernible above their belts. The parallel is important insofar as it shows the connection between the

costume and "ritual sports". The religious association of the latter can be proved by the fact that both boxing and bull-leaping are depicted on the steatite rhyton from Hagia Triada which was a cult implement.

It is noteworthy that contests of a ritual nature were depicted also on Egyptian wall-paintings. On fig. 77 such a contest involving two boys is represented in sequence. They are fighting and wrestling in the precincts of the temple of Thutmose III. To their right one sees the shrine with the sacred barge.

75. Boxing Children from B1.

76. Drawing of ivory pyxis from Katsamba, Crete, showing a bull hunter with a loincloth and knot similar to those of the Boxing Children.

77. Egyptian painting showing wrestling boys.

It remains to explain the intention behind the pictorial programme of the shrine (fig. 78). It should be noted that a band with ivy leaves runs above all paintings joining them into a coherent unit.

The common factor in all the frescoes is the idea of contest or competition which differs from serious conflict and only involves a test of strength. Interestingly enough ethologists apply the term "ritual competition" to animals to describe behaviour intended to demonstrate a "display of strength"; this is an apt description also for the sparring boys. The boxing contest is thus perceived in relation to nature. This makes sense in the light of the mentality of the Minoans and Therans who saw human society as an extension of nature and moved in harmony with it. The test of strength of young members of the human community is part of a larger order which applies to animals as well. We have seen that in the pictorial scheme of room 5 of the West House (fig. 17), animal life was used to reinforce the theme of aggression which was one of the messages in the paintings. Here the same method is used to express another idea: playful competition.

Monkey Frescoes

Anyone who has looked at the frescoes from Akrotiri will hardly have failed to notice the popularity of the monkey theme. Yet, they are not peculiar to Theran frescoes since there also exist several examples from Crete. One is the "Saffron Gatherer", from the palace of Knossos, in which Evans erroneously restored the monkey as a boy. Other monkeys exist on the frieze from the House of the Fescoes (fig. 61), which has already been mentioned in relation to nature scenes. Monkeys appear as part of landscape scenes in Crete and we shall see that this is also often the case on Thera.

It is possible to argue that the iconography of the monkey was introduced to Akrotiri from Crete; on the other hand, it has been claimed that a fossilized monkey skull has been found on Thera itself, which would indicate the presence of this animal on the island. Whatever the case may be, it is obvious that monkeys are used in similar thematic compositions on both Crete and Thera. In both places the conventional colour used is blue.

The significance of this animal was not clear until the restoration of the goddess fresco from Xeste 3 (fig. 40, chs. V, VI). There, a monkey is standing in front of the goddess as a privileged attendant. Taking this scene as a starting point, we could define the role of monkeys as that of special servants of the deity. The "Saffron Gatherer" from Knossos may well have been collecting crocuses in order to present them to a goddess who has not been preserved among the fragments. Another fragment from Thera supports this hypothesis. It was found in the area N. of the magazines, sector A, but the exact context is not indicated. On the fragment a monkey is depicted standing in front of an altar which is topped with horns of consecration and supported by columns ending in papyrus capitals (fig. 79). The monkey bends his arms in an attitude of worship; he is thus clearly shown as an adorant of the divinity in this case as well.

Several fragments depicting monkeys formed part of a frieze which was situated above the door of room 2 (ground floor) of Xeste 3 (fig. 51). Additional fragments, the relationship of which to the animals remains obscure, depict swallows courting or feeding their young in nests. Crocuses growing from rocks are visible below the swallows (fig. 47). This is significant because of the frequent association of monkeys with crocuses and birds. The interesting point about this frieze, however, has to do with the occupation of the monkeys who are engaged in human activities. Many of them are holding swords, whereas others play the lyre (fig. 80). Could they also be engaged in ritual contests in honour of the goddess who is depicted on the fresco of the neighbouring room 3? We cannot know the answer until the frieze is finally restored.

The special role of the monkey as a servant of the divinity may have been borrowed from Egypt where baboons are regularly shown as sun worshippers. In addition, however, the animal in question has many anthropomorphic characteristics which arouse the imagination. It is easy to think of them as demons who, although zoomorphic, are given human attributes in Minoan-Mycenaean iconography and appear as ministrants of the deity.

There was another room decorated with monkeys, room B6 of sector B. It contained "vessels of clearly religious use" according to the excavator so it also must have been a shrine. The fresco was in bad condition precipitated from above by a torrent which ran through that section of the settlement. The majority of the fragments depict monkeys, facing different directions and climbing on rocks. The latter are rendered in a stylized and somewhat bold design in blue, red and white patches. Bands of blue, red and white stripes and a spiral one between them finished the painting on the upper level. Together with the monkeys was found a fragment with the head of an animal which the excavator first identified as either bovine or canine, later deciding on the latter. This gave him the idea that the monkeys were pursued by a dog:

> "Here it looks as if the monkeys, pursued by hound are climbing in fear the abrupt rocks of the volcano. The leader of the herd brings the rear and turns his head towards the pursuers. Again, we are impressed by the deep knowledge the artist has of the monkeys' behaviour". Sp. Marinatos, *A Brief Guide to the Temporary Exhibition of the Antiquities of Thera*, p. 22.

This seems to be an erroneous reconstruction of the scene, however. The excavator mentions that some additional fragments were found together with the monkeys:

> We have also found some fragments depicting myrtles and other plants, possibly also the waters of a little ford, swallows flying in the sky... (Sp. Marinatos, *Guide...*, p. 21.)

These additional elements are crucial and change the nature of the composition which, indeed, appears to have been very close to the frieze from the House of the Frescoes (fig. 61). The following table illustrates the correlation of pictorial elements.

79. Drawing of a monkey in
front of an altar, found
in sector A.

80. Fragment of a monkey playing the lyre, from a frieze in Xeste 3.

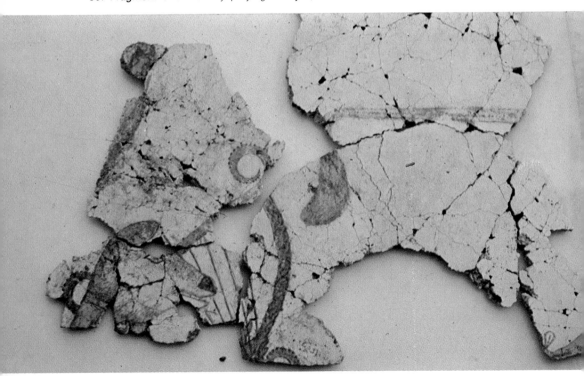

81. Monkey fresco from B6.

83. Attempt at a reconstruction of room B6.

Table 3

House of the Frescoes, Knossos	B6, Akrotiri
Monkeys	Monkeys
Myrtle	Myrtle
Swallow	Birds
Goats (not visible on fig. 60)	Head of goat(?)*
Crocuses	Crocuses

* This is what Sp. Marinatos interpreted as a canine head. Doumas tentatively identifies it as a goat and I agree because it fits the pictorial scheme.

The similarities can hardly be accidental and suggest that the compositions had very close affinities. On the basis of this I have attempted a reconstruction which is very tentative (fig. 83). It should be stressed that it is not based on fitting the very few fragments together, which is the only certain way of restoring, but on correlating the pictorial elements on the basis of analogy. Thus, it is the illustration on an idea rather than the product of laboratory work. Still, it is worthwhile attempting it in order to avoid misleading conceptions about the role of the monkeys in iconography. It will be remembered that not only do birds and other animals appear together with monkeys on the Knossian frieze, but that this is also the case with the monkey frieze from room 2 in Xeste 3. There swallows, courting and nesting, formed part of the composition. It is thus almost certain that the swallow, myrtle, and goat fragments, published in *Thera* II and III reports, were part of the monkey fresco.

I have placed the monkey and the landscape scenes on different walls because the rocks behind the monkeys are barren, without vegetation. It is, thus, unlikely that they would appear with other rocks from which plants grew. The monkey fresco, as restored, seems to have comprised two walls, the W. and N. ones. I have, therefore, placed the landscape scene on the E. wall. Fragments of rushes are published in *Thera* II (pl. 5.2). Since rushes are normally associated with waters and Sp. Marinatos mentions a ford, I have conjectured a small stream near which the plants grow. This is based on the observation that below the monkeys there are undulating bands with the characteristic hooklets which indicate waters. This river would presumably be continued on the abutting wall-painting. The swallow was found with the monkey fragments and is described as oversized by the excavator, so I have made it disproportionately large. In fact the birds from the Knossian frieze are also oversized.

If the restoration is valid, at least as an illustration of an idea, then the monkeys of B6 are depicted in association with the natural environment of the divinity: the spring landscape. Indeed, the swallows indicate the coming of spring as we have noted on other frescoes.

In conclusion, the monkey was picked out as a sacred animal by the Minoans and Therans. Whether depicted as a ministrant of the divinity or as populating her environment the message he conveys is religious.

CHAPTER X

Conclusions

The Themes of the Frescoes and Pictorial Formulae

The general impression one gets from Minoan and Theran art is that the frescoes exhibit an endless variety of themes, that there are virtually no repetitions and that there is striking originality in each composition. Compared with Egyptian art, where iconography is repetitive to the point of being wearisome, this is indeed true. It appears that in Crete the artist had more freedom to create and was less constrained by pre-existing patterns than his colleagues in Egypt. Yet, he too had to follow certain "ideological" guidelines. Upon close inspection, one realizes firstly that the actual themes of the frescoes are limited and secondly that there are overlaps between Cretan and Theran frescoes. All subjects revolve around festivals, rituals and nature scenes. This is a limited repertoire, within the framework of which, however, some variety of rendition was possible.

The repetition of themes, and especially the similarities between Minoan and Theran art, raises the question of transmission. How did Crete exert its artistic influence? Were there travelling artists or pattern books? I would be hesitant to accept the existence of the latter. As has been noted above, each composition is unique and it is very unlikely that it was copied from a pattern book. Once more the comparison with Egypt is instructive because some compositions are almost identical there. It is clear from Theran frescoes that the artists avoided repetition at all costs by varying the positions and costumes of the figures as much as possible. Daring experiments sometimes produced clumsy results which would have been avoided, had pattern books existed and been closely copied. Some figures from Xeste 3, for example, have feet which are too thick or hands which are too long in relation to the rest of the body. The artist was probably faced with the challenging task of creating an original painting within the framework of tradition. But how was the traditional theme transmitted? It is likely that there were travelling artists and it is also likely that the patrons, that is the priests who commissioned the paintings, were instructed in traditional themes. A comparison with oral poetry is instructive. Just as the poets and bards of the Homeric age had to compose traditional epics using formulaic language, so the artists and their patrons could create new compositions using traditional pictorial formulae. The application of this formulaic pictorial language gave them a solid framework in which to work without stifling their originality. There is little doubt that the formulae were dictated by the religious ideology of the Minoans. It is this predominance of religious themes combined with the architectural analysis that led me to the conclusion that the system at Akrotiri was theocratic.

Let us review some of the pictorial formulae of Minoan and Theran art. We have seen that certain motifs go together: lilies or crocuses with rocks and swallows, papyri and rushes with water or ducks, etc. (see also fig. 58). Conventions were used to indicate the elements in question. Rivers, for example, were rendered with undulating lines and hooklets; crocuses with three petals and two sets of stigmas, etc. The following table summarizes some of the observations on pictorial formulae.

Table 4

Signs	Types of Landscape	Animals	Plants
Hooklets	Rivers	Griffins, Ducks, Cats	Papyri, Reeds, Palms
Rocks	Rocky Landscapes	Goats, Monkeys	Lilies, Crocuses

Although these associations are not absolute, they are valid as rules of thumb and can be confirmed in many Aegean representations. The Nilotic scene on the dagger from Grave V, Mycenae, for example, shows a river landscape with cats, ducks and papyri; the river has the characteristic hooklets rendered by incision. On another dagger from Grave IV, a lion is chasing deer in a rocky landscape. The pictorial formulae are thus valid for a large corpus of Aegean art. This is worth keeping in mind when trying to establish differences between Minoan and Mycenaean works.

Art was thus a kind of language which could be learned and which conveyed the mentality of the people who produced it. Our task is to decipher this language and to understand its message.

The Meaning of Pictorial Motifs

All perception is selective. Therefore, the choice of certain motifs is meaningful and not random. I shall attempt to interpret the significance of some of the motifs that carried associations for the Minoans and Therans which are lost to us. The most obvious case is the frequent occurrence of crocus and lily. As has already been repeatedly stressed, these plants were chosen not only because of their beauty but because they were signs of the regeneration of nature in the spring and autumn. The same can be said about the swallow, the coming of which heralds the spring.

The associations conveyed by another bird, the duck, are less obvious although its appearance on the necklace of the goddess (fig. 49) shows that it was important. Its significance can be only understood in the light of Near Eastern and Egyptian parallels. It is clear that in both Egypt and Mesopotamia ducks were connected with fertility because they abound in marshes and waters. In both the above civilizations it was the waters of the river and the marshes which were responsible for the fertility of the soil. Unlike Crete, where the awakening of nature was dependent on warm temperatures and rain, in Egypt it was the rise of the Nile which fertilized the earth. Consequently, a cluster of visual and conceptual symbols was created revolving around waters and marshy landscapes. The occurrence of ducks, papyri, reeds and palms suggested water and fertility in the minds of the Egyptians. It is no accident that hunting in the marshes is one of the most beloved subject in tomb paintings of

Egypt since the Old Kingdom (fig. 50). In Mesopotamia plants and animals associated with water carried much the same connotations. A common Mesopotamian metaphor involves a comparison of the god of fertility or the king with a "datepalm planted beside a watercourse. A cedar, rooted beside waters..." (H. Frankfort, *Kingship and the Gods,* p. 311). In Mesopotamian literature there is an explicit connection between ducks and fertility. The pubic triangle of the fertility goddess Inanna is compared to "a stubble field on which ducks have been put out to be fattened..." (Th. Jacobsen, *The Treasures of Darkness,* p. 45).

To return to the Minoan and Theran world: although waters could not have been as important on Crete as in the Orient, they acquired the same significance under the impact of the Oriental civilizations. It is now explicable why a marshy landscape features in the pictorial programme of room 3, Xeste 3 on the upper floor (fig. 44); why ducks and dragon flies decorate the necklace of the goddess and why papyri appear in the shrine in the "Ladies' House".

The Order of Society and the Order of Nature

In the preceding chapters I have argued that the society of Akrotiri was organized around a system of shrines with a definite hierarchy among them and the latter were run by a ruling class which must have had priestly status. Economic, religious and everyday activities must have been intermingled to such an extent, that a distinction between the secular and the religious is irrelevant and artificial. The opposition between the sacred and the profane is a mental construct applicable to our own times and civilization, and attempts to impose it on this very different culture beclouds our judgement and obstructs our understanding.

The social hierarchy of Akrotiri is reflected in the art. Differentiations of costumes, hairstyles and position in the visual field are marks of social standing and importance. We have seen that kilts, tunics, shaggy skin-dresses and nudity for males are indicative of social position, youth and function (ch. IV). Short or long flounced kilts, a sari robe and different hairstyles indicate similar points about females (chs. V and VI).

The order of society was based on the order of nature. A harmonious relationship between the two was necessary and achieved by a series of festivals. In these the renewal of nature was celebrated in connection with events of social significance, such as victory, and creation of new roles (ch. V and VI). In this way the social order was integrated in the perennial order of nature. As H. Frankfort has stressed, it was the eternal and the recurring which impressed the ancients, not the ephemeral and transitory. Historical events implying singularity were meaningless because they were aberrations from the path of normalcy. But if they were part of a pre-existing mental and religious system, like victory of order over chaos, they could be integrated in it through festivals. It is no accident that historical events are absent from Theran and Minoan art and that political history was insignificant. There are no portraits, no leaders who stand out. The few faces on seals who have been regarded as princes or chieftains have been now shown by J. Betts to have been cast types representing priests. To this category falls also the leader of the fleet from the S. wall frieze with the ships from the West House (fig. 36).

It is interesting to compare Minoan and Theran art with that of the Greeks. The latter invented history, and it is no accident that they were interested in the phenomenon of change as we can see by studying the Ionian philosophers of the Archaic period. The singular event and the individual character interested the Greeks much more than it did the Minoans (although not as much as it interests us) and this perhaps is why they developed narrative art, literature, and last but not least, drama. True drama is out of place in a world where the eternal and recurring is what matters. We have seen that the potential dramatic moment of the *adyton* fresco from Xeste 3 (fig. 43) was lost because the tragedy of the girl is underplayed and because the scene lacks dramatic unity. Likewise, the bull-leaping scenes on Knossian frescoes loose in dramatic impact because the spectator acquires the impression that this is a recurring event, a ritual, where the individual actors do not matter.

In summary, Minoan and Theran art reveal the order of society and nature. In our world of rapid change and instability it is startling and comforting to get a glimpse, however inadequate, of a tradition where stability and repetition were the framework of human existence.

BIBLIOGRAPHY

Books cited in the text:

A. Evans, *The Palace of Minos at Knossos* I-IV (London 1921-36).
H. Frankfort, *Kingship and the Gods* (Chicago 1948).
    —. *Ancient Egyptian Religion* (New York 1948).
H. A. Groenewegen-Frankfort, *Arrest and Movement* (London 1951).
S. Hood, *The Arts in Prehistoric Greece* (Harmondsworth 1978).
Th. Jacobsen, *The Treasures of Darkness* (New Haven 1976).
K. Lorenz, *On Aggression* (New York 1966).
S. Marinatos, *A Brief Guide to the Temporary Exhibition of the Antiquities of Thera* (Athens 1971).
A. van Gennep, *The Rites of Passage* (London 1960).

Abbreviations:

AA	*Archäologischer Anzeiger*
AAA	*Athens Annals of Archaeology*
Burkert, *GR*	W. Burkert, *Griechische Religion der archaischen und klassischen Epoche* (Stuttgart 1977)
Delt	Ἀρχαιολογικόν Δελτίον
Ephemeris	Ἀρχαιολογική Ἐφημερίς
AJA	*American Journal of Archaeology*
AthMitt	*Athenische Mitteilungen*
BICS	*Bulletin of the Institute of Classical Studies of the University of London*
BSA	*Annual of the British School at Athens*
Doumas, *Thera*	Ch. Doumas, *Thera, Pompei of the Ancient Aegean* (London 1983)
Hood, *Arts*	S. Hood, *The Arts in Prehistoric Greece* (Harmondsworth 1978)
JdI	*Jahrbuch des Deutschen Archäologischen Instituts*
JHS	*Journal of Hellenic Studies*
KrChr	Κρητικά· Χρονικά

Nilsson, *MMR*	M.P. Nilsson, *The Minoan-Mycenaean Religion and Its Survival in Greek Religion* (2nd ed., Lund 1950)
Praktika	Πρακτικά τῆς ἐν Ἀθήναις Ἀρχαιολογικῆς Ἑταιρείας
PM I-IV	A.J. Evans, *The Palace of Minos at Knossos* I-IV (London 1921-36)
SCABA	*Sanctuaries and Cults in the Aegean Bronze Age,* R. Hägg and Nanno Marinatos eds. (Stockholm 1981)
TAW I-II	*Thera and the Aegean World* I-II, Ch. Doumas ed., (London 1978-80).
Thera I-VIII	Sp. Marinatos, *Excavations at Thera* I-VII (Athens 1968-76)
TUAS	*Temple University Aegean Symposium*

CHAPTER I. AIMS AND METHODOLOGY

For bibliography on Minoan religion see below, ch.II under "Shrines and Religion".

The older generation of Minoan scholars represented mostly by A.J. Evans (*JHS* 21 (1901) 99ff.) and A.W. Persson (*The Religion of Greece in Prehistoric Times,* Berkeley 1942) produced somewhat speculative but often intuitive interpretations centering around a vegetation goddess and her consort and "primitive" rituals. M.P. Nilsson's *The Minoan-Mycenaean Religion* (Lund 1927[1], 1950[2]) was a major breakthrough because of the systematic collection of the corpus of the archaeological evidence. A trend of scepticism runs through this book. Very important insights can be found in articles by F. Matz on Minoan epiphany, A. Furumark on the nature of Minoan deities, N. Platon about Minoan shrines and S. Alexiou on the goddess with upraised arms (see bibliography under "Shrines and Religion" for full references). B. Rutkowski's *Cult Places in the Aegean World* (1972), is a redoing of Nilsson with updated material on Minoan shrines. His work, systematic and invaluable as a handbook, suffers nevertheless from a certain overscepticism which, in the end, beclouds the picture of Minoan cult practices.

It is clear that the study of Minoan religion will advance further if it is fertilized by other disciplines. An excellent example of such an approach is the work of Ch. Sourvinou-Inwood who, in her use of structuralism, post-structuralism and semiotics, is coming up with very important results. See especially: "On the Authenticity of the Ashmolean Ring 1919.56", *Kadmos* 10 (1971) 60-69; "On the Lost "Boat" Ring from Mochlos", *Kadmos* 12 (1973) 149-58; and the forthcoming monograph on methodology and cult with two important essays: "Reading Dumb Images: a Methodology for Minoan Religion and Iconography" and "Renewal and Divine Return: a Minoan Ritual Reconstructed". For the origins of Minoan religion: P. Warren, "The Beginnings of Minoan Religion", in *Antichità Cretesi* (Levi-Festschrift) I, 1977, 137-147 and K. Branigan, "The Genesis of the Household Goddess", *Studi micenei ed egeo-anatolici* 8 (1969) 28-38.

Works on Egyptian religion which I found especially inspiring are H. Frankfort's *Kingship and the Gods* (Chicago 1948) and C.J. Bleeker's *Egyptian Festivals* (Leiden 1967), the former for attempting to capture Egyptian mentality, the latter for stressing cult practices rather than beliefs.

CHAPTER II. THE SETTLEMENT AND ITS SIGNIFICANCE

General Books on Akrotiri:	*Thera* I-VII; Sp. Marinatos, *Kreta, Thera und das mykenische Hellas* (München 1973); Ch. Doumas, *Thera;* Ch. Doumas, ed., *TAW* I-II.
On the Architecture of Akrotiri:	*Thera* I-VII; J. Shaw, "Akrotiri as a Minoan Settlement" in *TAW* I, 429-36; C. Palyvou, «Ὁ προϊστορικός οἰκισμός τοῦ Ἀκρωτηρίου Θήρας», Ἀρχαιολογία 1 (1982) 16-30.
On Minoan Architecture:	J.W. Graham, *The Palaces of Crete* (Princeton 1962); J. McEnroe, "A Typology of Minoan Neopalatial Houses", *AJA* 86 (1982) 3-19; D. Preziosi, *Minoan Architectural Design* (Berlin 1983).
	For a good example of architectural functional analysis applied to Mycenaean palaces see K. Kilian, "Pylos: Funktionsanalyse einer Residenz der späten Palastzeit", *Archäologisches Korrespondenzblatt* 14 (1983) 34-48. See also

Nanno Marinatos, "The West House at Akrotiri as a Cult Centre", *AthMitt* 98 (1983) 1-19.

On "Lustral Basins":

A.J. Evans, *BSA* 6 (1899-1900) 38ff.; J.W. Graham, *The Palaces of Crete* (Princeton 1962), 125ff.; N. Platon, "Bathrooms and Lustral Basins", *Europa, Festschrift für E. Grumach* (Berlin 1967), 236-45; S. Alexiou, «Περί μινωϊκῶν δεξαμενῶν καθαρμοῦ», *KrChr* 24 (1972) 414-34.

On Shrines and Religion:

A. Evans, "Tree and Pillar Cult", *JHS* 21 (1901) 99ff. and in *PM* I-IV; Ch. Picard, *Les religions préhelléniques* (Paris 1948); M. Nilsson, *Minoan - Mycenaean Religion* (Lund 1950); B. Rutkowski, *Cult Places in the Aegean World* (Warsaw 1972) and *Frühgriechische Kultdarstellungen,* AthMitt Beiheft 8 (Berlin 1981) with bibliography; N. Platon, «Τό ἱερόν Μαζᾶ καί τά μινωϊκά ἱερά κορυφῆς» *KrChr* 5 *(1951) 96-160;* «Μινωϊκοί θρόνοι», *KrChr* 5 (1951) 385-412; «Τά Μινωϊκά οἰκιακά ἱερά», *KrChr* 8 (1954) 428-83; A.W. Persson, *The Religion of Greece in Prehistoric Times* (Berkeley 1942); F. Matz, *Göttererscheinung und Kultbild im minoischen Kreta* (Wiesbaden 1958); A. Furumark, "Gods of Ancient Crete", *Opuscula Atheniensia* 6 (1965) 85-98; S. Alexiou, *Ἡ μινωϊκή Θεά μεθ' ὑψωμένων χειρῶν* (Herakleion 1958) = *KrChr* 12 (1958) 179-301; Ch. Sourvinou-Inwood, "On the Lost *"Boat "* Ring from Mochlos", *Kadmos* 12 (1973) 149-58; G. Gesell, *The Archaeological Evidence for the Minoan House Cult and its Survival in Iron Age Crete,* PhD dissertation 1972, Univ. of North Carolina, Chapel Hill (revised version forthcoming in *Studies in Mediterranean Archaeology);* E. Vermeule, *Götterkult, Archaeologia Homerica* III, Ch. V (Göttingen 1974); Ch. Long, *The Ayia Triadha Sarcophagus* (Göteborg 1974); R. Hägg and N. Marinatos eds. *Sanctuaries and Cults in the Aegean Bronze Age* (Stockholm 1981).

On Mesopotamia:

H. Schmökel, *Das Land Sumer* (Stuttgart 1956); S. N. Kramer, *The Sumerians* (Chicago 1963). A recent article reassessing the economy: B. Foster, "A New Look at the Sumerian Temple State", *Journal of the Economic and Social History of the Orient* 34 (1981) 225-241.

On Relations with Crete and Mycenae:

R. Hägg and N. Marinatos, eds. *The Minoan Thalassocracy, Myth and Reality* (Stockholm 1984). See especially Nanno Marinatos, "Minoan Threskeiocracy on Thera", 167-78 and R. Laffineur, "Mycenaeans at Thera: Further Evidence?", 133-39 in that volume. A series of articles deal with the interrelations.

From the point of view of the material evidence: Sp. Iakovidis, "Thera and Mycenaean Greece", *AJA* 83 (1979) 102; *contra* J.L. Davis, "Mycenaeans at Thera: Another Look", *AJA* 85 (1981) 69ff.; M. Marthari, *Ephemeris* (1980) 182-211; W.D. Niemeier, "The Master of the Gournia Octopus Stirrup Jar and a Late Minoan I A Pottery Workshop at Gournia Exporting to Thera", *TUAS* 4 (1979) 18-26.

From the point of view of paintings: S. Immerwahr, "Mycenaeans at Thera: Some Reflections on the Paintings from the West House", *Greece and the Eastern Mediterranean in Ancient History and Prehistory, Studies Presented to F. Schachermeyr* (Berlin and New York 1977) 173-91.

From the point of view of political control: F. Schachermeyr, "Akrotiri, the First Maritime Republic?" in *TAW* I, 423-28; Ch.

Doumas, "The Minoan Thalassocracy and the Cyclades" *AA* (1982) 182-210; idem, *Thera,* 129ff.

From the point of view of religion: Nanno Marinatos, "Minoan Threskeiocracy on Thera" in *Minoan Thalassocracy* (supra); G. Säflund, "Cretan and Theran Questions", *SCABA,* 189-208.

On the Destruction of Akrotiri from the Archaeological Perspective: Sp. Marinatos, "The Volcanic Destruction of Minoan Crete", *Antiquity* 13 (1939) 425-39; idem, *Some Words about the Legend of Atlantis* (Athens 1969); idem, "The Volcano of Thera and the States of the Aegean", *Proceedings of the 2nd Cretological Congress (1966)* I (Athens 1968) 198-216; A. Furumark, "The Settlement at Ialysos and Aegean History c.1550-1400 B.C.", *Opuscula Archaeologica* 6 (1950) 150-271; J.V. Luce, *The End of Atlantis* (London 1969); D. Page, *History and the Homeric Iliad* (London 1963) and idem, "On the Relation between the Thera Eruption and the Destructions of Eastern Crete, c. 1450 B.C." in *TAW* I, 691-98; W.D. Niemeier, "Die Katastrophe von Thera und die spätminoische Chronologie", *JdI* 95 (1980) 1-76; E.S. Ramage ed., *Atlantis: Fact or Fiction?* (Bloomington 1978); see also review by Nanno Marinatos in *Classical Journal* 75 (1980) 362-364.

From the Geological Perspective: A.G. Galanopoulos and E. Bacon, *Atlantis* (London 1969); D. Ninkovich and B. Heezen, "Santorini Tephra", in *Submarine Geology and Geophysics,* Colston papers 17 (Bristol 1965); H. Pichler and W. Schiering, "The Thera Eruption and Late Minoan IB Destructions on Crete", *Nature* 267 (1977), 819-22.

CHAPTER III. THE ROLE OF WALL-PAINTINGS IN THE BRONZE AGE

For the traditional approach of Minoan art as decorative: H. Hall, *The Decorative Art of Crete in the Bronze Age* (Philadelphia 1907); F. Schachermeyr, *Die minoische Kultur des alten Kreta* (Stuttgart 1964). S. offers a penetrating analysis of Minoan art in his chapter "Kunst und Dekoration", pp. 179-221, which, however, adheres to the traditional view. On the contrary, H. A. Groenewegen - Frankfort in her book *Arrest and Movement* (New York 1951), which was published earlier, addresses seriously the question of ritual function of paintings. This is all the more interesting because she approached Minoan art from an Oriental perspective and saw Crete as part of the E. Mediterranean world. A basically religious function of murals is accepted by S. Hood, *Arts* and M. Cameron in *TAW* II, 317; Nanno Marinatos, "The Function of the Theran Frescoes", in *L'iconographie minoenne, Bulletin de Correspondance Hellénique,* Suppl. XI (forthcoming).

For Egyptian art: H.A. Groenewegen - Frankfort (supra); H. Frankfort, *Kingship and the Gods.*

For art and ritual: K. Lorenz, *On Aggression* (New York 1966) 73.

On Minoan/Cycladic Painting in general: Bibliography in S. Hood, *Arts,* 283ff.

CHAPTER IV. PICTORIAL PROGRAMMES: THE WEST HOUSE

On the Frescoes of the W. House: *Thera* V, 17-20, 41-44; *Thera* VI, 19-31; Nanno Marinatos, "The West House at Akrotiri as a Cult Centre", *AthMitt* 98 (1983) 1-19; Ch. Doumas, *Thera,* 82 ff.

On Pictorial Programmes: L. Morgan, *BICS* 28 (1981) 166 and "Theme in the West

House Paintings at Thera", forthcoming in *Ephemeris;* R. Hägg, "Pictorial Programmes in Minoan Palaces and Villas", in *L'iconographie minoenne, Bulletin de Correspondance Hellénique,* Suppl. XI (forthcoming). M. Cameron in *TAW* II 317, talks about an overall theme of fresco decoration at Knossos relating to the mountain goddess.

For a good example of pictorial programme analysis from Assyria see I. Winter, "The Program of the Throneroom of Assurnasirpal II", in *Essays on Near Eastern Art and Archaeology in Honor of Ch. K. Wilkinson* (New York 1983) 15-32. About the paintings in the palace of Mari: Y.M. Al-Khalesi, *The Court of the Palms: A Functional Interpretation,* Bibliotheca Mesopotamica 8 (Malibu 1978), especially chs. IV and V.

On the Young Adorants (Fishermen):

Thera VI, 23, 25; J. Sakellarakis, *AAA* 7 (1974) 370-90; M. Benzi, *Prospettiva* 10 (1977) 3-15, correctly identifies the figures as initiates. For parallels of shaved heads from Crete: E. Sapouna-Sakellaraki, *Proceedings of the 4th Cretological Congress* (1976) 1,2 (Athens 1981) 490, 503; Nanno Marinatos, *AthMitt* 98 (1983) 3. Recently A. Peatfield has studied the hairstyles of Minoan figurines from peak sanctuaries and has come to the conclusion that most of them have shaved heads with sculp locks. Some scholars think that shaved heads in Theran art denote youth. In addition to those mentioned in the text see G. Säflund in *SCABA,* 203, n. 69 *a* and fig. 26; Ch. Doumas, *Thera,* 85.

For initiation practices the classic work is A. van Gennep, *The Rites of Passage* (London 1960).

On the Miniature Friezes:

Thera VI, 38-44. The most extensive analysis has been written by L. Morgan in her dissertation (forthcoming by Cambridge University Press). See also L. Morgan-Brown, "The Ship Procession in the Miniature Fresco", in *TAW* I, 629-44; idem, "The West House Paintings", *BICS* 28 (1981) 166, idem, "Theme in the West House Paintings at Thera", forthcoming in *Ephemeris.*

The literature on the subject is large. For further bibliography see Nanno Marinatos, *AthMitt* 98 (1983) 2, n.2; only a small selection will be listed here.

TOPOGRAPHICAL IDENTIFICATION OF TOWNS: D. Page, "The Miniature Fresco from Akrotiri, Thera", Πρακτικά τῆς Ἀκαδημίας Ἀθηνῶν 51 (1976) 136-52; G. Gesell, "The Town Fresco of Thera, a Reflection on Theran Topography", *Proceedings of the 4th Cretological Congress (1976)* I, 1 (Athens 1980) 197-204; P. Warren, "The Miniature Fresco from Akrotiri, Thera and Its Aegean Setting", *JHS* 99 (1979) 116-29.

RELIGIOUS INTERPRETATION: L. Morgan-Brown, *TAW* I, 629-44; G. Säflund, "Cretan and Theran Questions", *SCABA,* 189-208; Nanno Marinatos, "The West House at Akrotiri as a Cult Centre" *AthMitt* 98 (1983) 1-19.

RECENT ARTICLES: E. Davis, "The Iconography of the Ship Fresco from Thera", in *Ancient Greek Art and Iconography,* ed. W.G. Moon (Madison 1983) 3-14; A. Raban, "The Thera Ships: Another Interpretation", *AJA* 88 (1984) 11-19; R. Laffineur, "Early Mycenaean Art: Some evidence from the West House in Thera", *BICS* 30 (1983) 111-112.

	See also bibliography to ch.II under the heading "Relations with Crete".
On Minoan Dress:	Sp. Marinatos, *Kleidung, Haar und Barttracht, Archaeologia Homerica* I, Chs. A-B, 21-32; E. Sapouna-Sakellaraki, Μινωϊκόν Ζῶμα (Athens 1971); G. Korres, «Παραστάσεις προσφορᾶς ἱερᾶς ἐσθῆτος καί ἱεροῦ πέπλου», *Proceedings of the 4th Cretological Congress, (1976)* I, 2 (Athens 1981) 558-88 (with bibliography); S. Immerwahr, "The People in the Fescoes", in *Minoan Society*, O. Kryszkowska and L. Nixon eds, (Bristol 1983) 147-148.
On the Priestess:	*Thera* V, 41-43; E. Sapouna-Sakellaraki, «Οἱ τοιχογραφίες τῆς Θήρας σέ σχέση μέ τήν μινωϊκή Κρήτη», *Proceedings of the 4th Cretological Congress (1976)* I, 2 (Athens 1981) 499-501; L. Morgan-Brown, *TAW* I, 640. For parallels of her dress: *PM* IV, 405. Egyptian priestly garments in A. Erman - H. Ranke, *Ägypten* (Tübingen 1923) 337. Red ear: there is a figurine at Malia to which Prof. J.C. Poursat has kindly alerted my attention, see *Fouilles exécutées à Mallia. Le Quartier Mu II, Etudes crétoises* XXVI (Paris 1980) 103 and fig. 139. There is also a fresco fragment from Pylos in M. Lang, *The Palace of Nestor* II (1969) 76, pl. 24 and col.pl.C.
On the Cabin Frescoes:	*Thera* V, 41; VI, 35; L. Morgan, *TAW* I, 641 and *BICS* 28 (1981) 166; M. Shaw, *AJA* 84 (1980) 167-79; Nanno Marinatos, *AthMitt* 98 (1983) 5.
About the Ritual and Windows of Appearance:	Windows of appearance in Crete have been conjectured by J.W. Graham, *AJA* 74 (1970) 231-39; I. Beyer, *Der minoisch-mykenische Palasttempel* (Freiburg-Berlin 1981) pl. 39; R. Hägg, "The Reconstruction of the West Facade of the Palace at Knossos" in *The Function of the Minoan Palaces, Proceedings of the 4th International Symposium at the Swedish Institute, Athens 1984* (forthcoming). A proof of their existence is the so-called "house-model" from Archanes which must rather have been a shrine. Note especially the steps leading to a balcony which must have been a "balcony of appearances" with parallels in Egypt. See A. Lembessi, *Ephemeris* (1976) 12-43.
	Purification rituals connected with windows of appearance have been conjectured for the palace-temple complex at Medinet Habu: R. Stadelmann, *Mitteilungen des Deutschen Archäologischen Instituts Kairo* 29 (1973) 221-42. The "shower-room" next to the throne-room of the king in the palace is considered a preparation room by S. and it would make a good parallel to room 4a in the West House at Thera.

CHAPTER V. PUBLIC FESTIVALS ON THERAN FRESCOES

Minoan Festivals:	F. Schachermeyr, *Die minoische Kultur des alten Kreta* (Stuttgart 1964) 135-39; Nanno Marinatos, "Public Festivals in the West Courts of the Palaces", in *The Function of the Minoan Palaces, Proceedings of the 4th International Symposium at the Swedish Institute, Athens 1984* (forthcoming).
Egyptian Festivals:	H. Frankfort, *Kingship and the Gods* (Chicago 1948); C.J. Bleeker, *Egyptian Festivals* (Leiden 1967).
Greek Festivals:	K. Kerényi, "Vom Wesen des Festes", *Paideuma* 1 (1938/40) 59-74; W. Burkert, *Griechische Religion der archaischen und klassischen Epoche* (Stuttgart 1977) 163-66; W.H. Parke,

	Festivals of the Athenians (London 1977); E. Simon, *Festivals of Attica: an Archaeological Commentary* (Madison 1983).
On the Festival on the Miniature Friezes:	Bibliography to Ch. IV.
On the Lion as a Symbol of Aggression:	O. Keel, *The Symbolism of the Biblical World* (New York 1978) 85-87. The Mycenaeans also used it in this way as an emblem of power: E. Vermeule, *The Art of the Shaft Graves of Mycenae* (Cincinnati 1975) 41.
On Egyptian Victory Festivals:	C.J. Bleeker, *Egyptian Festivals* (Leiden 1967) 92ff., with further references.
On the Bearded Type:	J. Betts, "The Seal from Shaft Grave Gamma - A Mycenaean Chieftain?" *TUAS* 6 (1981) 2-8. B. argues that such "portraits" characterize priests rather than chieftains.
On the Crocus Gatherers:	*Thera* VII, 34-38 and col. pls. A-K; I. Douskou, "The Crocus of Santorini", *TAW* I, 582; Ch. Doumas, *Thera*, 106-108; idem, *Praktika* (1980) 295.
On the Thesmophoria and Kalligeneia:	L. Deubner, *Attische Feste* (Berlin 1965) 53-60. D. does not think virgins took part in the festival although Burkert, *GR* 365, thinks it likely. See also W. Burkert, *Homo Necans* (Berlin 1972) 248, 288; M. Detienne, "Violentes eugénies" in M. Detienne and J.P. Vernant, *La cuisine du sacrifice en pays grec* (Paris 1979); W.H. Parke, *Festivals of the Athenians* (London 1977) 87-88.

Parke thinks that the Skira and the Thesmophoria are related festivals taking place in the spring and fall respectively. The postulated festival depicted on the walls of Xeste 3 may have also included two seasonal stages compressed in one.

See also R. Parker, *Miasma: Pollution and Purification in Early Greek Religion* (Oxford 1982) 82-83.

CHAPTER VI. INITIATION, VEGETATION AND SACRIFICE: THE ADYTON FRESCO OF XESTE 3

On *Adyta:*	See bibliography in ch. II. In particular A.J. Evans, *BSA* 6 (1899-1900) 38ff.; S. Marinatos, "The Cult of the Cretan Caves", *Review of Religion* 5 (1941), 130. M. suggests that "Lustral basins" or *adyta* are formalized versions of caves. See also the comment in Nilsson, *Minoan-Mycenaean Religion* (Lund 1950) 94. Further: *Thera* VII, 25ff.; G. Gesell, *The Archaeological Evidence for the Minoan House Cult and its Survival in Iron Age Crete* (Ph. D. dissertation Chapel Hill 1972) 106ff. A cultic character of *adyta* is denied by B. Rutkowski, *Cult Places in the Aegean World* (Warsaw 1972) 229-31, who accepts a sacred character for only two cases.
On the Altar Fresco:	A similar fresco composition depicting a priestess walking towards an altar depicted on an E. wall was found in the fresco room in the Cult Centre at Mycenae. A good picture in E.B. French, *SCABA,* 47 fig. 13.
On Blood Libations:	Nanno Marinatos, "Minoan Sacrificial Ritual", forthcoming.
On the Relation of Myth to Ritual:	The classic work for the Near East is S.H. Hooke, ed., *Myth, Ritual and Kingship* (Oxford 1958). A more contemporary approach in C.J. Bleeker, *Egyptian Festivals* (Leiden 1967) 11-15.

For Greek religion J. Harrison, *Prolegomena to the Study of Greek Religion* (Cambridge 1922) and idem, *Themis* (Cambridge 1927). The one-to-one relationship between myth and rite is no longer accepted by many scholars but a relationship does exist. See W. Burkert, *Structure and History in Greek Mythology and Ritual* (Berkeley 1979).

On Initiation Patterns:

A. van Gennep, *Rites of Passage* (London 1960). A painting depicting analogous rites to those in the fresco from Xeste 3 is the one from the Villa of the Mysteries in Pompei. There also there is a veiled girl who looks towards a sacred object or action. See e.g., B. Andreae, *The Art of Rome* (New York 1977) pls. 27-31. M. Cameron, in *TAW* I, 582, connects the saffron gathering from the Xeste 3 fresco with initiation.

Initiation, Seclusion, Death, etc:

B. Malinowski, *Magic, Science and Religion* (New York 1948) 21. M. mentions as common features of initiation seclusion, ordeals culminating in mutilation, ordeals associated with the idea of death and rebirth. See also Th. Reik, *The Creation of Woman* (New York 1960). For the Greek ritual of the Arrhephoria W. Burkert, *Hermes* 94 (1966) 1-25; and idem, *Homo Necans* (Berlin 1972) 169-73.

On Eleusis:

G. Mylonas, *Eleusis and the Eleusinian Mysteries* (Princeton 1961); K. Clinton, *The Sacred Officials of the Eleusinian Mysteries, Transactions of the American Philosophical Society,* New Series 64 (Philadelphia 1974).

A reconstruction of the rites in W. Burkert, *Homo Necans* (Berlin 1972) 274-327.

CHAPTER VII. LANDSCAPE SCENES

On the botanical study of frescoes:

M. Möbius, "Pflanzenbilder der minoischen Kunst in botanischer Betrachtung" *JdI* 68 (1933) 1-39; O. Rackham, in *TAW* I, 755-84.

On the Hagia Triada Fresco:

L. Pernier and L. Banti, *Guida degli scavi italiani in Creta* (Rome 1947) 31; *PM* I, 538, fig. 391; W.S. Smith, *Interconnections in the Ancient Near East* (New Haven 1965) 77; S. Hood, *Arts,* 52ff.

On the Phylakopi fresco:

Excavations at Phylakopi in Melos conducted by the British School in Athens (London 1904) 72ff.; *PM* I, 544-7 and III, 4lf., fig. 26; S. Hood, *Arts,* 53.

Seal from Routsi:

S. Marinatos - M. Hirmer, *Kreta, Thera und das mykenische Hellas* (München 1973) pl. 232.

On the House of the Frescoes:

PM II, 431-67; M. Cameron, *BSA* 63 (1968) 1-31; S. Hood, *Arts,* 51-52.

Lilies Fresco:

Thera IV, 49-51; S. Hood, *Arts,* 55; Nanno Marinatos, "The Function of the Theran Frescoes", in *L'iconographie minoenne, Bulletin de Correspondance Hellénique,* Suppl. XI (forthcoming).

Papyrus Fresco:

Thera V, 39. S. Marinatos argues that the plant is pancratium lily but this cannot be so because the iconographical form is clearly that of papyrus — except that papyri normally do not have leaves even on Theran frescoes. The anomaly can be explained by the unfamiliarity of the artists with this particular plant. That papyrus can grow in the Aegean has been argued by P. Warren, *JHS* 99 (1979) 23.

For a collection of iconographical motifs of papyri see *PM* II, 477 and W.D. Niemeier, *Die Palaststilkeramik von Knossos*, Archäologische Forschungen 13 (Berlin, forthcoming). The latter scholar has also shown that "hooklets" indicate rivers and waters.

CHAPTER VIII. DRESSING THE PRIESTESS: THE FRESCOES OF THE LADIES

On the Room of the Ladies:
Thera V, 11-15, 38-41; VI, 8-11. Ch. Doumas, *Thera*, 81-82, expresses doubts as to the repositories belonging to the room of the frescoes, but repositories, sealed below the floor, are attested at Knossos, *PM* I, 463ff.

On costumes:
S. Peterson, "A Costuming Scene from the Room of the Ladies on Thera", *AJA* 85 (1981) 211; Ch. Televantou, «Ἡ γυναικεία ἐνδυμασία στήν προϊστορική Θήρα», *Ephemeris* (1982) 112-35.

M. Cameron has come to conclusions similar to mine about a costuming scene in his restoration of the "jewel fresco" (*PM* I, 526, fig. 383).

CHAPTER IX. ANIMALS AND HUMANS: THE ANTELOPES, BOXING CHILDREN AND MONKEY FRESCOES

On Antelopes and Boxing Children:
Thera IV, 46-49; Ch. Doumas, *Thera*, 78-79; Sp. Marinatos, *AAA* 4 (1971) 407-12.

For the restoration:
Note *Thera* IV, pl. 5lb where the outline of one antelope next to the window is preserved *in situ*.

On Boxing:
Parallels from frescoes: *PM* I, 498 ff. (possibly from East Hall); M. Shaw, "The Miniature Frescoes of Tylissos Reconsidered" *AA* (1972) 171-88. From seals: *PM* II, 500 ff.

On the Ritual Nature of Boxing:
Burkert, *GR*, 174.

Monkeys:
Thera III, 63-64. Note especially the comments on p. 64 on which I base my restoration:

"It seems that other kinds of animals were also represented in the same composition. A head, fragmentary, of course, may be that of a dog or a bovine. Swallows fly in the air. One of them is almost entirely preserved (pl. 62.2 and col. pl. B 1). Finally, great fresco fragments were already found in 1968 in the same neighbourhood showing floral motifs of myrtle and rush".

Compare the aforementioned myrtle fragments (*Thera* II, pl. 6) with those from the House of the Frescoes at Knossos, *PM* II, 458, fig. 270.

Monkeys from the House of the Frescoes have been related to Egyptian paintings by Evans, *PM* II, 448-50. M. Cameron's restoration was published in *BSA* 63 (1968) 3ff. See also N. Platon, «Ὁ κροκοσυλλέκτης πίθηκος», *KrChr 1* (1947) 502-24.